CAREFREE CANOEING
IN FLORIDA

A GUIDE TO TRAILS AND OUTFITTERS ON FLORIDA'S SCENIC WATERWAYS

Brooksie and John Bergen

Gulf Publishing Company
Houston, Texas

Gulf Publishing Company
Book Division
P.O. Box 2608 □ Houston, Texas 77252-2608

10   9   8   7   6   5   4   3   2   1

Library of Congress Cataloging-in-Publication Data

Bergen, Bernice Brooks, 1924–
    Carefree canoeing in Florida / by Brooksie and John Bergen.
       p.   cm.
    Includes bibliographical references (p.) and index.
    ISBN 0-88415-171-9
    1. Canoes and canoeing—Florida—Guidebooks.   2. Florida—
Guidebooks.   I. Bergen, John.   II. title.
    GV776.F6B47   1997
    796.1′22′09759—dc21   97-5439
                                                CIP

DISCLAIMERS

The authors make no claim that the maps presented in this book are accurate or drawn to scale. All maps are intended merely to approximate the locations of the waterways and outfitters described in this book. We hope they will give some idea of the scope and geography of the state of Florida.

The authors have selected from the myriad waterways in Florida that they personally feel are best suited to the skills and interest of recreational canoeists. They have pinpointed those offering scenery most descriptive of each particular section of Florida. They wish to make it clear that they make no endorsement or representation of companies or organizations listed in this book. They assume no responsibility for outdated information or information inadvertently omitted, such as addresses, fees, names, phone numbers, and hours. The omission of any canoe outfitter, state park, or waterway does not imply that such facilities lack merit. Revisions and supplementary information may be included in future printings. Please advise the Publishers if you wish to offer a comment.

LISTEN TO THE QUIET

Listen to the quiet,
You city clones,
Metropolis-molded,
Transistor-trained,
Noise numbed.
Do you hear the hush?
Do you feel it
Seep into your soul,
A soft cocoon
Of stillness?
Listen to the quiet.
Let it speak to you.
Do you hear it?
Did you know
It was still there?

Bernice Brooks Bergen

GIRL SCOUTS OF AMERICA PADDLING SONG

(chanted in time to paddle strokes)
Peace, I ask of thee, oh, River
Peace . . . Peace . . . Peace.
When I learn to live serenely
All my cares will cease.
From the streams I gather courage,
Visions of the days to be,
Strength to lead and Faith to follow,
All are given unto me.
(Repeat)

Anonymous

CONTENTS

PREFACE

You can experience the joy of paddling Florida's scenic waterways even if you don't own a canoe, have never managed one, or don't have considerable strength, endurance, or athletic ability. This book specifically lists waterways that are accessible by means of canoe liveries, and includes maps and simple directions for reaching them. We've designated those excursions that offer "potty-stops" along the way, and those that lack them. A brief history accompanies each waterway along with rental fees, schedules, concessions, and nearby attractions; and we have rated the routes individually as to difficulty and scenic beauty based on our own impressions. The tips and suggestions we've compiled are the result of our personal experiences and the mistakes we've made ourselves along the way.

Carefree Canoeing in Florida is written for paddlers who prefer to be pampered, who don't want to store or maintain their own equipment. It's geared toward weekend athletes and family boaters who have no desire to stagger across the shallows bearing the weight of unwieldy canoes on their backs. And it's a must for nature lovers, photographers, or amateur bird watchers.

Because we've been Pampered Paddlers ourselves for more than twenty years and have found it difficult to pinpoint, in a single publication, the existing canoe trails that offer rentals, we've prepared an easy-to-read but comprehensive guide. You won't have to wade through academic rhetoric to get the information you want. It's the handbook we've always wished we had handy.

We've paddled more than 300 miles, driven more than 13,000 miles from the southern peninsula of Florida to the Panhandle to select those canoe trails we feel best represent each ecologically diverse section of the state. There are countless waterways throughout Florida including hidden ones unknown to all but a few, but not all of them navigable unless you're an "elite" canoeist: one who owns his own gear and is competent enough to manage under any conditions.

We've chosen not only those streams, rivers, springs, and creeks that are accessible to the general public by means of liveries, but those we found to be the most interesting, the most canoeable, and the most "user friendly."

Like the Indians, alligators, and other threatened wildlife that have retreated to the last refuges preserved for them, many of us seek that same elusive peace and quiet. It's still available. You don't have to be a world traveler and you don't have to be wealthy. All you need is this book to give you access to a world that's right at your doorstep . . . a world of myriad waterways, many you never knew existed, that wind in and out of tall river grasses, through swamps, around clumps of mangroves, beneath towering cypress trees, cedars and palms, or dense canopies of oaks.

Florida's canoe trails meander through forests that shelter ospreys, bald eagles, turtles, snakes, and countless varieties of wading birds and waterfowl. Colorful wildflowers explode from the undergrowth, and lily pad gardens float lazily on the water's surface. Alligators poke their huge, horny heads out of murky, coffee-colored streams and bark to unseen mates. Otters, manatees and fish of all kinds roil the waters, leaving silvery trails. Now and then you can spot a deer or a wild boar crashing through the underbrush. And it's all yours to enjoy from the convenience and safety of your rented canoe, paddling with your rented paddles.

When you've chosen a specific trail, one that appears to meet your own requirements, refer to the maps for directions and, once arrived, let the affable and able-bodied hired help get you launched. From that moment on, you are a canoeist, albeit, a pampered one, free to let go and Listen to the Quiet.

Brooksie and John Bergen

ACKNOWLEDGMENTS

Special thanks are due to the following: Peter L. Koenig and Shirley Hummel, photographers and friends; Frank and Jan Lapniewski of Wilderness Canoe Adventures, Wimauma (Frank is former President of the FACLO, Florida Association of Canoe Liveries and Outposts); Ted Greenwald and Mary Ellen Towers of The Great Outdoors Inn, High Springs; Posey's Restaurant and Motel, Panacea; Jack, Esther, and Mike and Linda Sanborn of Adventures Unlimited, Milton; Jim Hollis of Hollis' River Rendezvous, Mayo; Tocoi Fish Camp and Lodge, Tocoi; Everglades Outpost and Ivey House, Everglades City; Dianna Collier, my agent, for her hospitality; and Gulf Publishing Company, which made all this possible.

The Little Manatee River. Photo by Bernice Brooks Bergen.

WATERWAYS IN FLORIDA

WATERWAYS IN ALPHABETICAL ORDER

How To Use This Book

The general ratings for each waterway included in this guide were determined by the authors' personal assessments of the concessions, quality of equipment and service, scenery, and difficulty. A rating of "X," for instance, is what we considered a mediocre trail; "XX" was pleasurable; "XXX," highly enjoyable; "XXXX," superior or spectacular. In some cases we regarded a waterway as a "pampered paddler's plus," one of several particularly oustanding excursions. These ratings do not necessarily reflect those of our fellow "pampered paddlers." You, the reader, can make the final judgment.

Each waterway in this guide is identified by number in the alphabetical list to waterways on page xiii and on the master map on page xii.

The authors wish to make it clear that they make no claim that the map presented here is accurate or drawn to scale. It is intended merely to approximate the locations of the waterways described in this book, for the convenience of our readers. We hope it will give some idea of the scope and the geography of the state of Florida.

INTRODUCTION

PADDLING WITH THE ACA

For those of you who may feel intimidated and a little embarrassed by your lack of skill when confronted by more experienced paddlers, take heart from the following excerpt from *Paddler*, December 1994, "Paddling with the ACA" (American Canoe Association) by Jeffrey Yeager, Executive Director:

"As with most sports, paddling has developed its own hierarchy . . . a pecking order if you will . . . particularly in the minds of those who live and breathe nothing but paddling," Yeager writes.

"It's probably fair to say that many of paddling's self-proclaimed 'elite' view themselves (begat, evidently, directly by the river-gods) at the very top of this pyramid, followed by all other 'serious' paddlers in descending order of skill level and quality of equipment owned.

"In the minds of some private boaters," Yeager continues, "paddlers who don't own their own equipment . . . the patrons of liveries and outfitters . . . really aren't paddlers at all. In the minds of some, these folks aren't even part of the hierarchy, or, worse yet, are viewed as a nuisance by 'real boaters' who want free and unobstructed use of the river.

"In response to those who harbor such feelings, the American Canoe Association politely says, 'HOGWASH!' We believe that everyone who wants to paddle has an equal right to use and enjoy our waterways for that purpose, and also has an equal responsibility for preserving and protecting those waterways. Ownership of your own equipment should not dictate access to our natural resources.

"The fact is that most of America's paddlers rely on the nation's 2,500-plus liveries and outfitters to experience the joys of paddlesports. According to the National Association of Canoe Liveries and Outfitters (NACLO), an estimated 10 million individuals patronize liveries and outfitters each year in the U.S. This means that more than 90 percent of all paddling is done by livery and outfitter customers, not by private boaters."

TIPS FOR CAREFREE CANOEING

- Because of its murderously hot summers, canoe season in Florida is, to our way of thinking, October to May. "Off-season," you're on your own. Avoid sunstroke, heat exhaustion, and stinging insects the best you can.
- In general, aim for an early morning departure. The weather is cooler, the water is calmer, and your energy level is higher.
- If you haven't done much paddling, pick an easy trip for a start (this manual pinpoints them) to test your endurance and attention span.
- Pick your companion carefully. An hours-long, cramped ride in a confining, easily tipped canoe is a true test of compatibility. Be aware that canoe trips are joyous occasions for nature lovers, not party animals.
- Store gear in the center of the canoe or distribute it evenly. Take your positions carefully in the bow and the stern on the cross seats, keeping in mind that the one in the bow usually calls the signals, the one in the stern does most of the steering. Be sure to get that straight before you begin.
- If you're a solo canoeist, it's best to sit or kneel with knees wide in the center of the canoe, with your back and hips braced against the center thwart. If your knees are vulnerable due to injury or mileage, bring a cushion. We're told they will soon be unavailable at most liveries.
- Wear a waterproof watch. You tend to lose all sense of time on the water. And it's wise to take along a compass. Trips that don't provide shuttle service to or from launching or destination sites necessitate careful planning. Allow approximately 2 miles per hour under normal conditions, which, to the occasional canoeist, should be "ideal" only.
- Don't bring a radio, please. Most people are there to listen to the call of wildlife, not heavy metal. Respect regulations that often prohibit alcoholic beverages, firearms, and pets.
- Because of its precarious design, a canoe is no place for rough-housing, drinking or amorous advances. If you decide to change

positions at any time with your partner, be ready for a tricky and complicated set of maneuvers called, not inappropriately, "The Paddlers' Ballet."

- It hardly seems necessary to remind you not to toss waste overboard. We once saw a canoe overturned by a pair of militant canoeists who spied its occupants littering a pristine waterway. While not all canoe-trail vigilantes use such drastic means of calling attention to "water hogs," they are watching you.

- Don't wear perfume. It's nothing but a love potion for every sex-crazed insect in the vicinity no matter what the season. Do bring repellent just in case. Florida bugs are unpredictable. Wear a hat or visor, and always use a sunscreen even in cooler weather or on cloudy days.

- Layer clothing. Even casual canoeing causes blood you never knew you had to circulate more intensely. You may have to shed a jacket or sweater, then replace them in the event of a sudden change in Florida's fickle weather. The layer closest to the skin should have the power to draw moisture away from the skin and disperse it into the air or the next layer of clothing. The middle layer should insulate, the outer, provide protection from rain or other unpleasant and unforeseen elements. Sneakers or specially designed canoe shoes are best for feet.

- Respect "Posted" signs. No one likes trespassers. If nature calls, there are usually spots along the shore which are public domain. You should never canoe without small amounts of toilet paper discreetly tucked into your waterproof bag.

- Like the animals, please cover or remove all evidence of your presence.

- Those who like to bring their own lunch should be on the lookout for convenient sandy areas to land the canoe, carefully disembark, and pull it up after you. You can use the cushions for seats. If you prefer eating in the canoe, pull up against a log or other barrier to keep the craft from tipping or floating away.

- Include a plastic bag for your own refuse, and if you'd like to do your bit in keeping the waters clean, pick up cans, bottles or other garbage within easy reach.

- While it's not prudent to exchange small talk with an alligator, you needn't fear them if you keep your distance. Don't feed them, talk to them, or wave to them. They're people-shy, turning into predators only at night . . . so we're assured.

- Stay to the right of powerboats. They're intrusive and noisy, but some waterways allow them. Most respect the "No Wake" or "Manatee Area" signs. Turn the bow into the wake if you encounter an unmannerly pilot.
- Stay on the designated canoe trails unless byways are specifically marked.
- We once got hopelessly lost in the maze of channels in the Everglades . . . something that happens often, we're told. If you wander into an inviting channel along the way, keep landmarks in mind . . . an unusually shaped tree or log, for instance; use your compass; listen carefully to descriptions of canoe trails, especially designated drop-off or pick-up spots. From the water, it's often difficult to spot those not identified by visible signs.
- If, by chance, your canoe overturns, stay with it. It floats, even if you don't. Most waterways are not uniformly deep. Push your craft (and your gear) into a shallow area before you try to right it, or find a hammock of low branches on which to overturn it to empty it of water. It's not too hard to do. We ought to know! It's a good idea to invest in waterproof cases for cameras and anything else you want to protect. Again, we ought to know!
- Bring a snack. It's surprising how hungry you get on the water. And include soft drinks or water, of course.
- Canoe weekdays, if at all possible, to avoid crowds both on the highway and on the water. Always call ahead to assure that the livery is open, what the hours are, and to check on the tides and weather conditions. There may be changes at some of the facilities by the time this book is in print.
- Be advised that most state parks do not offer the complete services supplied by privately owned outfitters, so be prepared to do some of your own hauling and lifting if you choose their facilities.
- Take a camera (in your waterproof container) to capture some of the most memorable moments of your life . . . gliding silently across Florida trails untouched by civilization . . . entering a world where time stands still.

POTTY-STOP POINTERS FOR PAMPERED PADDLERS

No guide to Florida's canoe trails would be complete without addressing the sudden call of nature when surrounded by nothing but wilderness. The necessity for potty-stops in the Florida underbrush, sometimes referred to as "gator country," strikes fear in the hearts of the uninformed. It should be noted from the start that the Florida alligator, although territorial, preys mostly at night, preferably on small, helpless game, and generally splashes quickly out of sight at the first approach of a human. The same goes for other wildlife.

With that bugaboo hopefully laid to rest, here is a practical approach for the problem of relieving oneself in the Florida wilds:

1. Check this guide carefully for references to potty-stops. Take into consideration those trails that don't have them, and drink liquids and time your journey accordingly.
2. As we've suggested previously, always include several lengths of toilet paper in your waterproof bag, your body-bag, or in the pocket of your jeans, shirt, or jacket.
3. Pick a sandy strip upon which to beach your canoe, one that looks lonely enough to preclude an embarrassing confrontation. In our case, we take turns posting a lookout while the other tends to the business at hand.
4. Be careful to obey "No Trespassing" signs. There's enough public property to fill your needs. And retreat as far as possible from the water, or at least 150 feet from any park or campsite, for obvious sanitary reasons.
5. Need we remind you to check the spot you've picked for poison ivy? Or prickly plants?
6. We've said it before, but it bears repeating: Don't leave signs of your ministrations behind. If you don't have a small spade handy in your gear to dig a hole, remove a rock, bury the toilet paper in the depression, and replace the rock. Or scoop a layer of soil over any droppings. Even a thin layer helps decompose paper, and

within a few days nature will take over and purify any waste. Admittedly, men have the advantage here, but there's no excuse for a woman to become untidy just because she's not in her own home. Here, the outdoors is everyone's home.

John and Brooksie Bergen on the Little Manatee River. Photo by Shirley Hummel.

TO YOUR HEALTH

C anoeing is one of the oldest forms of transportation, dating from the time men hollowed out logs to cross the waterways, to hunt and fish, or to haul supplies. Along with rowing a boat, it achieved popularity as a recreation in the early 1900s, remaining a favorite pastime until the advent of motor boats. But recently, it has been recognized as a viable form of exercise.

There's something about being afloat on one of Florida's rivers that opens a window on a new and more peaceful world of suspended time and endless space, being one with nature. Rivers and their tributaries are the planet's arteries, carrying its lifeblood, water, someone once said. Their essence can literally improve your own lifeblood!

With the current jogging and high-impact aerobics craze and its attendant joint maladies and stress fractures, it's comforting to know that paddling a canoe at a steady rate can offer a fitness alternative guaranteed free of trauma to various parts of the body. The water's resistance to the measured strokes of a paddle creates an exercise comparable to a steady walking pace, both offering activities that can be enjoyed for long periods of time without undue stress or fatigue. All the strokes involved, including the use of the paddle as a rudder, involve the muscles in the upper arms and shoulders, forearms, wrists, and hands. Even the lower back and abdominal muscles are put into play, and there are definitely cardiovascular benefits.

Physicians agree that canoeing, an activity that anyone can master if geared to his or her age and physical condition, can improve muscle tone, has alleviated various aches and pains brought on by lack of exercise, and in some cases has been a panacea for lower back pain. *Carefree Canoeing in Florida* will help you decide which trails are most beneficial for your own physical needs. British researchers, we're told, have discovered that woods and greenery might have "powerful preventive and curative influences," and that contact with nature "improves self-esteem, increases altruism and heightens a sense of being alive." We can personally attest to the overall sense of well-being, serenity and improved health canoeing provides. And it's noncompetitive. You can set the pace yourselves. Travel the waterways to escape civilization and its pressures for a few hours, to meditate, reflect, and enjoy the sight, sound, feel, smell, and taste of nature at its best.

Granddaughter Trecy and John Bergen in Oscar Scherer State Park.

FLORIDA STATE PARKS OFFERING CANOE RENTALS

Florida is a bigger state than most people assume. We found that out after traveling over 13,000 miles to canoe the waterways listed in this book. Each region has its own unique qualities — the Panhandle has a southern backwoods flavor with moss-draped oaks; the coastal regions feature vast bays, blue seas and white sandbars; central Florida is most famous for its caverns and crystal-clear springs. But all have one thing in common: splendid state parks. Use this listing to help you select the park nearest you by referring to the specific cities on your atlas.

BLUE SPRING, Orange City
(904) 775-3663

COLLIER-SEMINOLE, Naples
(941) 964-0375

DE LEON SPRINGS, DeLeon Springs
(904) 958-4212

JONATHAN DICKINSON, Hobe Sound
(407) 546-2771

FLORIDA CAVERNS, Marianna
(904) 482-9598

FORT COOPER, Inverness
(904) 726-0315

GOLD HEAD BRANCH, Keystone Heights
(904) 473-4701

HILLSBOROUGH RIVER, Thonotasassa
(941) 987-6771

HONTOON ISLAND, DeLand
(904) 736-5309

HUGH TAYLOR BIRCH, Ft. Lauderdale
(305) 564-4521

JOHN U. LLOYD BEACH, Dania
(305) 923-2833

LAKE KISSIMMEE, Lake Wales
(941) 696-1112

MACLAY GARDENS, Tallahassee
(904) 487-4556

MANATEE SPRINGS, Chiefland
(904) 493-6072

MYAKKA RIVER, Sarasota
(941) 361-6511

OCHLOCKONEE RIVER, Sopchoppy
(904) 962-2771

O'LENO, High Springs
(904) 454-1853

OLETA RIVER, North Miami
(305) 947-6357

OSCAR SCHERER, Osprey
(941) 483-5956

PAYNES PRAIRIE, Micanopy
(904) 466-3397

JOHN PENNEKAMP CORAL REEF, Key Largo
(305) 451-1202

ST. JOSEPH PENINSULA, Port St. Joe
(904) 227-1327

TOMOKA, Ormond Beach
(904) 676-4050

WEKIVA SPRINGS, Apopka
(407) 884-2009

GUIDED TOURS OF FLORIDA WATERWAYS

....

Guided canoe trips or tour boat excursions offer alternatives to those who are not physically able to manage a canoe themselves but still want to experience the pleasure of exploring the wilderness splendor of the many scenic rivers in Florida. Some even give you the option of dipping an oar yourself now and then. Others involve package weekends that include personalized service. The following offer various types of guided excursions:

CANOE ADVENTURES, INC.
2058 Wild Lime Drive
Sanibel, FL 33857
(941) 472-5218

Janie and Mark "Bird" Westfall have organized a guided, educational canoe trip around picturesque Sanibel Island that has been operating since 1978. They use a 20-foot canoe that can carry five passengers at a time, including Mark, who acts as guide. In this manner, they can transport people, who for some reason or another cannot paddle a canoe themselves, out into the wilderness areas. Their customers include not only the elderly, but also people who are sight-impaired, have heart problems, even people who need to be carried into the canoe. The trips are also ideal for families with young children, or for parents who don't feel comfortable navigating their own canoe with their children on board. In addition to the large canoe, they provide two 17-foot canoes that can carry three people per canoe. This limits their total number to eleven passengers per trip, but they do take as few as two passengers on occasion. The Westfalls do not have a facility, but take reservations by phone, then meet their clients at specified locations, depending on the particular scheduled length of the excursion and the area covered. Passengers are guided through the J.N. "Ding" Darling National Wildlife Refuge on Sanibel; down the Sanibel River; to the island of Buck Key off CapTiva Island; or to Mound Key, off the coast of Fort Myers Beach.

FLORIDA ADVENTURES
John Judy
1073 W. Country Club Circle
Plantation, FL 33317
(305) 584-7669

John Judy offers a different type of service: a personalized canoe weekend (or longer) with meals freshly cooked and prepared by his staff. He sets up two- and four-person tents and issues all canoeing gear. Consider this an Americanized safari. You can choose either primitive camping along the river, or base camping at the local parks that offer full facilities and day-tripping on the rivers. It's your call! A typical trip for 16–20 persons costs $95 a head. Shuttle service is provided, and the excursions are guided, of course. Complete instructions for beginners and for those who wish to improve their paddling skills are part of the deal. John's adventures cover the Withlacoochee, Peace, Alafia, Arbuckle, Wekiva, Rock Springs, Ocklawaha, Silver, Juniper Springs, Santa Fe, Ichetucknee, and Loxahatchee rivers. For more detailed information on specific dates and the river of your choice, call or write to him.

NOTE:

Neither of the above-mentioned enterprises was initially included in this book, but we felt they deserved special consideration. Both called, in response to our query letters, regarding their particular services. These are only two examples of guided tours supplied by many of the liveries. For other liveries which offer guided tours, call those described in this book. Most of the state parks offer them, too.

PART I

PANHANDLE

BUCKHORN CREEK

Many seldom-traveled backroads and hidden waterways of Florida's Gulf Coast are omitted from publications describing canoe trails in the Sunshine State. Rich in history and legend, the Big Bend section of Northern Florida, also known as the Apalachee Coastal Region, remote, unspoiled, forgotten, is one most people have never had the pleasure of exploring. The area was once occupied by warlike Indian tribes who used its rivers for hunting and fishing. Long ago, Aztecs and Toltecs followed the Gulf in their dugouts to the safety of the sheltered Wakulla River region; others, like the Timucanas, Seminoles, and Creeks arrived by land. Near the famed Wakulla Springs, Spaniards explored and conquered, and Indian mounds and excavated artifacts are mute evidence of long-vanished tribes.

In 1539, St. Marks became the second permanent town in Florida. In 1865, the Battle of Natural

Bridge was fought north of Wakulla Springs. The victory by the Confederates made Tallahassee the only state capital east of the Mississippi to remain unconquered by the Union Army. In 1836, the first railroad line, mule-driven cars that traveled over iron strips, linked Tallahassee to St. Marks. Its "passenger car" was a box with two wooden benches seating a total of eight passengers. Signs of the old railroad bed can still be spotted at Newport.

The Wakulla River region abounds in natural riches, and presents a pristine, uncrowded beauty unique to this part of Florida: small, secluded beaches accessible only by boat; tiny creeks winding through tidal marshes; interwoven strands of rivers, wetlands, beaches, springs, estuaries, and forests abounding with wildlife. As a result of our query letters, we happened upon one of those little-known waterways in that historic section of the state often referred to as the "Real Florida," and a gentle, scholarly man who is spearheading a drive to preserve the quality of life and the history that surrounds the communities not too many miles south of bustling, metropolitan Tallahassee.

Barry Laffan, a displaced native of Queens, New York, is an anthropologist who has traveled and worked worldwide, and who now lives with his attorney wife, Joanna, on the Ochlockonee Bay in a remote little fishing village called Panacea. To aid the economically depressed area, Laffan is promoting what he calls "ecotourism." He and others are hoping to attract visitors to replace the town's declining forestry industry and the commercial fishing fleet which locals consider an "endangered species" in spite of what is perceived as a successful seafood industry. Ecotourism is Laffan's buzzword for the "sportsman's paradise" he envisions for the area. He and dedicated people like the managers of POSEY'S RESTAURANT AND MOTEL, local attorneys, and civic and government organizations are in the process of developing what may be the nation's first "boat trail" along the coastlines of Ochlockonee Bay and St. Marks River. Called the Apalachee Coastal Archeological Boat Trail, its intention is to link selected historical sites in the area and will include sections of the Wakulla, Sopchoppy, Tallahassee, and Ochlockonee rivers. By the time this book is in print, the plan should be in effect, offering a first to our readers: a unique package deal encompassing heretofore unexplored canoe trails and places of interest.

CANOE RENTALS

GULFCOAST EXCURSIONS
203 Mashes Sand Road
Rt. 1, Box 3201
Panacea, FL 32346
(804) 984-5895

From Tallahassee, take Highway 363 south to Highway 98, turn west on 98 through the town of Panacea. Just before the bridge, turn east off 98 on to Mashes Sand Road, Route 372, and continue east until you reach number 209, the number on the mailbox. It's a little difficult to spot Laffan's home at the end of a winding drive to the bay. His canoe livery is just getting off the ground, but by the time you read about it here it should be a well-organized and comprehensive venture, a unique way to explore rivers, lakes, wetlands, bays, springs, beaches, islands, historic sites, and forests. His package deals, operating out of a number of different sites, are arranged beforehand at his home, so advance reservations and schedules must be made ahead of time. They will include, according to the wishes of the client, paddling by canoe or kayak, sailing, cruising, swimming, picnicking, photographic excursions, fishing, hiking, and just relaxing. "Tailor-made" marine, wildlife, archeological, and scenic tours of the area's coastal wilderness will be available. Laffan stresses flexibility as to time, location, and mode, and he will organize overnight accommodations and prepare take-along meals if desired. He specializes in group outings. Subject to change, rates are: Canoes, $12 for a half-day, $18, full-day; guide service, $20 per hour; special pick-ups and drop-offs, $25 maximum. He hopes to have a more comprehensive shuttle service in time. At present, he also arranges trips on the dark waters of the Sopchoppy River, which flows through the Apalachicola National Forest; Otter Lake, and Ochlockonee Bay, both of which are wide expanses and inclined to be choppy if it's windy.

CONCESSIONS

As we've stated, Laffan operates out of his home, so it's advisable to bring your own cooler unless you've arranged for one of his picnic lunches. If you're desperate, he'll allow you the use of his bathroom. The nearby Wakulla Springs State Park, St. Marks Wildlife Refuge, and Ochlockonee State Park have all manner of concessions, restrooms, and snack stands, as well as nature trails and tourist attractions. Wakulla Springs, a vast preserve offering elegant accommodations, swimming, and guided tours, should top your list of must-sees.

THE TRAIL

We follow Laffan's car to one of the remote locations that acts as his headquarters for a canoe trip. A ten-minute ride leads us to four battered canoes chained to a bar stashed away in the wilderness on the edge of a scenic creek. He unlocks one, brushes off the leaves, and helps us carry it to the dock below. We slide the craft down the wooden steps to the water and paddle toward a tropical paradise. Forewarned, we're heavily slathered with insect repellent which keeps the flies at bay for the most part, but they still create an annoyance. Nothing, however, can dispel the beauty of this crooked little waterway, a black, silent mirror.

We paddle past a cluster of river homes and boat sheds, saw grass islands, and into a designated wildlife refuge. Various hardwoods form a background for the giant pines and cypress trees lining the water's edge. The Buckhorn is a shallow tidal creek with a total absence of current, and the stillness is so vast, we find ourselves whispering. The huge fish that churns the water at the side of the canoe is called an "orange-breasted brim," we learn from a lone fisherman, and they appear often and without warning. This trip is a sleeper! We seem to be totally alone here . . . no people, no boat traffic, no litter. It's the best kept secret in Florida. If you want a wild and scenic river that's still easy to paddle, this is it. Soon, the creek seems to close in, becoming more heavily canopied, and we can see patches of deep, glowing crimson on the sandy bottom, indicating the concentration of tannic elements. Once we pass under the bridge that spans the highway, we realize it would have been better to have turned back. We paddle a little further and find ourselves ducking under foliage and branches, and scrambling past almost impassable deadfalls. When the twists and turns become too difficult, we reluctantly head back. The journey to the bridge and back, we figure, would have taken us almost two hours; short but idyllic, and a totally new experience. (A note of caution: A potty-stop in the brush proved disastrous for me. Ten days later, small patches of poison ivy erupted at my waist and an unmentionable area, which proves it's best to take care of certain ablutions before the onset of any canoe trip in general. Try to limit potty-stops to sandy areas.)

GENERAL RATING: XXX
DIFFICULTY: EASY
SCENERY: EXCELLENT

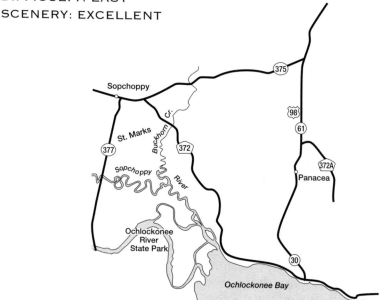

WAKULLA RIVER

Wakulla is a Seminole-Creek word variously translated as "breast of life," "mystery," or, more commonly, "mysteries of strange water." The original name for Wakulla was "Tah-ille-ya-aha-n," meaning "where the water flows upward like the rays of heavenly light out of the shadows of the hill." This lyrical translation might refer to the "Wakulla Volcano," a mysterious pillar of smoke in the swamp that was first reported by early Spanish explorers. Or it might allude to the river's primary origin in a spring of magnificent proportions, and the tribes' possible discoveries of fossilized remains of extinct Ice Age giants in its many caves.

Legends abound concerning the Wakulla. Since 1850, scientists have indeed identified the bones of at least ten prehistoric mammals. The springs were also reputed to contain mysterious curative powers. Later, the Creeks referred to the river as "WAH-kola," meaning "loon," for two species of the bird which wintered there. Through the years, the name was simplified to Wakulla, meaning "mystery." Wakulla Springs is the world's largest and deepest spring, a giant hole spouting 350,000,000 gallons of water a day from a single fissure. Although the waters reach a maximum depth of 185 feet, objects on its bottom are clearly visible and appear far closer. The springs are located in the Edward Ball Wakulla State Park approximately 15 miles south of Tallahassee, and about midway between the towns of Apalachicola and Perry in Wakulla County.

Ball, a grammar school dropout, lived to become one of the richest financiers in the country. During Florida's legendary land boom in the 1920s, the most enterprising braved swamps and mud slides, insects, and tropical wilderness to scout the area for future development and ensuing riches. Two of these visionaries were Alfred I. DuPont, and his brother-in-law and business manager, Edward Ball. The dense forests of stately Florida pines provided ideal fodder for the turpentine and logging industries, but Ball was looking for land conducive to growing pulpwood when he found the springs. Overwhelmed at once by its beauty, he determined to somehow preserve the area, and found the means when his 4,000-acre woodland tract, known as "Ed Ball's private zoo," was purchased by the government in 1986. It continues to be maintained as a wildlife refuge and public attraction. The uniqueness of the springs and the lucidity of the water made it an ideal setting for several motion pictures, including the Tarzan series.

CANOE RENTALS

TNT HIDEAWAY
6527 Coastal Highway
Highway 98 & Rt 2, Box 4200
Crawfordville, FL 32327
(904) 325-6412

OUZT'S OYSTER BAR AND CANOE RENTAL
Highway 98 East & Rt. 4, Box 6812
Crawfordville, FL 32327
(904) 925-6448

There's a decided lack of commercial ventures in this remote section of Florida, and these two friendly liveries, only a mile or so apart, often exchange customers. We decided on TNT for our excursion on the Wakulla as recommended by POSEY'S, the modest but comfortable little motel in the nearby town of Panacea, which accommodated us for two nights. The aptly named TNT HIDE-AWAY is located approximately 18 miles south of Tallahassee on Highway 98, and can be reached by traveling south on SR 363 to the intersection of SR 267. Turn right (west) and then left at the fork to 365. Continue for two miles and take a left down a dirt road just before the bridge that spans the river. Miz Gretchen, small, lean, and weathered, has been part of the family-owned and operated business since 1976. The facility is open year-round, seven days a week from sunup to sundown. Rates for two persons are $11 for each canoe, for a minimum of 4 hours, and there's a 50-cent charge for each life jacket. An all-day trip for two persons is $17 for the canoe and fifty cents for each life jacket. Fishing is permitted with the proper licenses, but firearms and treble hooks are not. To date, there are no kayaks available.

CONCESSIONS

Miz Gretchen's little frame office, perched on stilts at the water's edge, carries the bare necessities for canoeing and fishing: ice, snacks, and cold drinks. It's a short paddle, but bring your own snacks if you feel you need them. Also, take advantage of the primitive but clean rest rooms as there are no convenient potty-stops. Be warned that even at the end of April, when we took this trip, the "no-seeums" were a real problem in this part of Florida. Miz Gretchen sells insect repellent and sunscreen if you forget to bring your own, and they're a must along with a wide-brimmed hat or visor. We also recommend wearing sneakers because the sand in these parts clings to everything. Lodging, picnicking, swimming, hiking, and sight-seeing can be found at the famous Wakulla Springs State Park located on Highway 267 just ten miles north of TNT HIDEAWAY.

After our canoe trip, we ate in the little luncheonette in the gift shop of the historic old Wakulla Springs Lodge in the park. The shop features a 60-foot-long marble-topped soda fountain that once served as the bar. Built in 1937, the lodge, former home of Edward Ball, is furnished with antiques to retain the stately ambience of yesteryear. The old Moorish archways and iron grillwork are typical of the Spanish-style architecture so popular in those days. The big attraction in the cavernous lobby is the glass-encased, stuffed carcass of "Old Joe," the resident alligator, who, according to local lore, lived to be 200 years old, weighed 650 pounds, and measured 17 feet. Supposedly harmless, Old Joe was "murdered" in 1966 by unknown hunters, and is still mourned. During the summer, visitors can enjoy swimming and snorkeling in the crystal clear waters of the springs, or tour the waters on one of the glass-bottomed boats to meet Henry, the Pole-Vaulting Fish. Other attractions include the nearby OCHLOCKONEE RIVER STATE PARK, and ST. MARKS WILDLIFE REFUGE.

THE TRAIL

Beginning your canoe adventure at TNT HIDEAWAY is an outing designed for the "young, elderly, and the entire family," states their brochure. Miz Gretchen advises us that taking advantage of the cool breezes in the a.m. is best for this trip as she helps us slide our canoe down the sandy ramp into the water. It's a leisurely six-hour round trip paddle. Because of the almost total lack of current and the broad, uncluttered expanse of water, there's no need for a shuttle, although Miz Gretchen tells us they are considering adding one. After we pass under the highway's overpass where a few fishermen are anchored, and quaint, rustic river homes on stilts, we seem to be alone on the Wakulla. Signs posted at frequent intervals warn against disturbing the manatees, but a power boat overtakes us, slowing as it passes, then immediately speeding up again in apparent disregard of the gentle mammals. It's a reminder that boat traffic does exist here even on a Monday, so stick to weekdays if you can. The cypress trees are a splendid sight here, lining the shore, guarding their ghostly dead, with blossoming dogwood adorning their sturdy limbs like frilly, frivolous white collars. Occasional palms, looking slim, elegant, and alien, peer between their ranks. After we're underway about fifteen minutes, the river becomes narrower and even more scenic with the added interest of several lushly vegetated islands. The hardwood forest contains three state champion trees: the Sassafras, American Beech, and American Basswood. The shallow marshes on the river provide a haven for wading birds, a veritable "birding mecca." A great blue heron swoops through the underbrush on shore as we pass, and the constant shrill call of anhingas accompanies sightings of wood ducks, great egrets, cormorants, and countless other wading birds. We don't see a bald eagle today, but we do spot a lone osprey soaring overhead. We're told alligators, raccoons, deer, wild boar, and otters frequent these surroundings, but it's a little early in the season, and only various species of turtles are evident today. Rays of sunlight pierce the dark, clear waters to reveal seagrass swaying with the current, delicate tendrils whose existence is threatened by boat propellers, dredging, and pollutants. We try not to dwell on this sad decline as we pass the many quaint birdhouses erected in the trees. These are called kestrel boxes, built to imitate tree cavities favored by the small falcon known as a "sparrow hawk." We take time to explore the many winding, narrow bayous and coves along the way, and are awed by the sight of a giant blue heron on guard, standing motionless while her young offspring flits nervously back and forth. We end our paddle at the Highway 365 bridge where a fence protects the Wakulla Springs Wildlife Refuge. Respectful of the barrier, we pull up on a sandy ramp to stretch our legs and rest, then paddle back, enjoying the return as much as the first half. It's a six-mile, three-and-a-half-hour round trip of sheer pleasure, and the steady paddling gives us an opportunity to increase our heart rates. As our chapter on canoe fitness states, this kind of mild exercise is perfect for cardiovascular enhancement. Miz Gretchen is there to greet us, but we pull the lightweight canoe back into place without her help.

The Wakulla, almost entirely litter-free, thanks to TNT's periodic cleanup, is one of the panhandle's most popular lazy rivers, and not to be missed.

GENERAL RATING: XXXX
DIFFICULTY: EASY
SCENERY: EXCELLENT

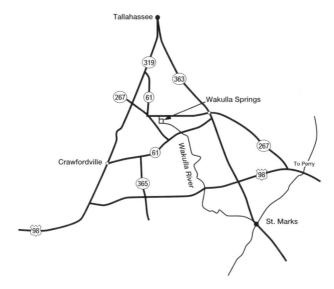

Wakulla River

ST. MARKS RIVER

The beautiful river and its equally scenic tributary, the Wakulla, are the two northernmost crystalline, spring-fed rivers in Florida. The St. Marks, located in Leon and Wakulla counties, is in the Florida Panhandle, 20 miles south of Tallahassee in the town of Newport on Highway 98. Its name most probably derives from a Spanish Fort, the San Marcos de Apalache, which occupied the site in 1718 and changed hands several times before it was taken by the Confederate Army during the Civil War. The St. Marks River is perhaps best known for being the site of the battle of Natural Bridge in 1665, during which the Confederate Army defeated Federal forces in their attempt to capture Tallahassee. The true natural bridge, formed by St. Marks as it passes underground at that point, is the site of a small state memorial. From there, it continues at the St. Marks Spring and flows for about eleven miles, merges with the Wakulla River, and winds on out to the Gulf of Mexico.

The town of Newport has its own interesting history. A once-flourishing port with large stores, warehouses, piers, a turpentine distillery, cotton press, steam saw, and grist mill, Newport and the nearby town of Magnolia attracted traders as well as visitors who sought the cures of the nearby mineral springs, and the excellent hunting and fishing. At its peak, Newport had about 1,500 inhabitants, and for ten years remained the fifth-largest town in Florida. The advent of railroads caused its decline and the demise of the water-borne cotton trade. Newport has slipped back into relative obscurity, a sleepy, scattered little community like so many in the vicinity. All that remains of Magnolia is a cemetery deep in the woods.

CANOE RENTALS

OUZT'S OYSTER BAR AND CANOE RENTALS
Highway 98 East
Rt. 4, Box 6812
Crawfordville, FL 32327
(904) 925-6448

TNT HIDEAWAY
6527 Coastal Highway
Highway 98 & Rt 2, Box 4200
Crawfordville, FL 32327
(904) 925-6412

Newport's present "hub of activity" is Ouzt's, a family-operated livery located below the St. Marks River Bridge. Canoe rentals are handled by the Ouzts inside their rustic little Oyster Bar. Take Highway 98 west from Perry and continue west to Newport until you reach the spot where the St. Marks River crosses Highway 98 from north to south. Ouzt's is situated on a dirt road below the highway on the west side of the river and the north side of Highway 98. There are a limited number of canoes, rented out on a first-come, first-served basis, so the proprietors recommend advance reservations. Open seven days a week from sunup to sundown, which seems to be standard in these parts, Ouzt's offers a seven-mile trip upriver from their launch to the Natural Bridge at the rise of the river and back; or a three-mile trip downriver to the town of St. Marks and back.

Canoes rent for $9 per canoe for two people, with life jackets, for up to four hours. The all-day rate is $15 per canoe with an additional charge of fifty cents, for some reason, for the life jacket. Fishing on the river is permitted, but a license is required in fresh waters. The owners assured me that by the time this book is in print they'll have a shuttle available for those who don't want to take the seven-mile round trip.

CONCESSIONS

Ouzt's looks rustic and primitive with its cracker-style decor, but its owners know what fishermen and canoeists need. You can buy ice, snacks, all the usual supplies, and even a takeout food order for your canoe trip. When we entered, one of the owners was preparing her special smoked mullet dip. They also serve what they claim are the world's best oysters and smoked mullet, bacon-wrapped shrimp, and shrimp pie. Prices are reasonable. You can get soft drinks and beer there, but no wine. There's a big screened pavilion for picnics and dancing, and on Thursday and Sunday evenings they offer "some of the finest music in north Florida." Their latest venture is a St. Marks

River Festival in May featuring arts and crafts, live entertainment, food and beverages, and games. The nearby Wakulla Springs State Park, St. Marks Wildlife Refuge, and Ochlockonee State Park are places worthy of exploring, and the charming restaurants on the river are noted for their fine dining.

THE TRAIL

Not many publications regarding canoe-friendly rivers mention the St. Marks, one of the largest tidal rivers, but we find it to be one of the most enjoyable. After we're issued our paddles and life jackets, our attendant simply points us to the spot on the river where he has set our canoe, and we're on our own, carrying our gear to the take-out spot. There's no pampering in the panhandle, it appears. There are no cushions, and sitting on life jackets,.. we've found, is uncomfortable, so bring your own cushion if you feel the need, a hat or visor, and that indispensable insect repellent. Unlike the Wakulla, the St. Marks is sparsely populated, and there's little boat traffic. We paddle upstream against a barely perceptible current through water that is as black and still as any we've encountered, and just as pure. Cypress trees dominate, as is usual in the Panhandle, and there's a profusion of magnolias, palms, and hardwoods, river grasses, and other tropical, lowland vegetation. The St. Marks River is pristine, unlittered, its waters abounding with marine life, a variety of wading birds, and wildlife. Seeping springs, swamps, and small tidal creeks present an everchanging panorama as we glide silently and easily on the river that was once one of the main trade arteries in the area. Today it's placid, mirroring the trees that line its shores, winding and twisting its way, closing in on itself at intervals. There are numerous, convenient sandy potty-stops along the way, so it's no problem to navigate the seven-mile round trip.

We've already had our lunch at Wakulla Springs, so we snack on a power bar and take a few sips of bottled water. It's so quiet you can hear the wind in the trees like distant waterfalls, and the splash of our paddles, and the calling of birds. At the Natural Bridge, we turn back, a paddler's dream trip with a cool breeze fanning us, the current at our backs, and the splendid, unspoiled vista before us. A large flock of snow-white kites explodes suddenly from the bushes, scatters, rests on the topmost branches at intervals, and soars on ahead of us. We're tired when we return, pull our canoe up on shore, and carry the gear back . . . we've canoed all morning and all afternoon, after all . . . but Charles Ouzt's kind offer of a cold beer refreshes us. We feel we've explored a river that offers a rental unknown to most canoe enthusiasts, an entree to one of the best wilderness excursions.

GENERAL RATING: XXXX
DIFFICULTY: EASY
SCENERY: EXCELLENT
A PAMPERED PADDLER'S PLUS!

St. Marks River

HOLMES CREEK
(CYPRESS SPRINGS)

Holmes Creek appears to originate near the Alabama-Florida border northeast of a town called Bonifay, but is little more than an unnavigable trickle until the flow from Cypress Springs, two miles north of the town of Vernon in Washington County, transforms it into one of the most popular canoe trails in the area. Local lore has it that the creek was originally called the "Okchaihatchee" (River of the Okchais, a Creek sub-tribe). The name was later changed to honor a Creek Indian Chief named Holmes, whose father was a "white man." Chief Holmes, known by his Indian name of Ekanchatte Mico, and his followers fled to the Spanish-occupied land for refuge in 1814, and built a little village on the site called Holmes Village. Chief Holmes, a formidable foe, was eventually killed by United States troops sent to Holmes Valley by General Jackson. Advertised as the largest spring in Washington County, producing close to 90 million gallons of water a day, Cypress Springs is Florida's newest dive site. The spring flows southerly .03 miles where it enters Holmes Creek, and at lower water levels can be larger than Holmes Creek itself.

CANOE RENTALS

CYPRESS SPRINGS CANOE TRAILS, INC.
P.O. Box 716
Vernon, FL 32462
(904) 535-2960

Take Highway 10, take exit 17 to Highway 79, and go south toward Vernon. Turn left on Cypress Springs Road and continue to Cypress Springs. You'll see the signs. "We were the first ones here aside from the Indians, the last tribe being the Creeks," says Harold Vickers, who is co-owner and operator of Cypress Springs along with his wife, Linda. The Vickers have been in business here since 1983, and have established a reputation for friendly service and entree to one of the most scenic canoe excursions in the state. By the time this book is in print, they will have enlarged their general store to include a deli, a complete line of books including ours, additional souvenirs, snacks and supplies, along with the usual dive shop and fishing essentials. The Vickers rent out 100 hard plastic, serviceable Coleman canoes, and a small number of kayaks. Canoes rent for $10 per person for a three-mile trip involving one-and-a-half hours paddling time; $15 per person for a 10-mile trip or 4 hours. A three-mile tubing trip, 4-5 hours, costs $8 per person.

CONCESSIONS

When the Vickers' new store and office is completed, it will include restrooms and an inviting picnic pavilion overlooking the water. But the real attraction in these parts is the Springs, which were first explored by Woody Jasper in 1985. It has since been opened to the public, and contains a cavern that expands to a large room with a maximum height of 14 feet. The Vickers do a booming business with divers. The area offers excellent camping and picnicking facilities.

THE TRAIL

After arranging a pick-up time, we follow Harold, the canoe atop his shoulders, down the walkway that leads through a swampy area to the water's edge. After he sees us safely afloat, we paddle the short distance to the springs to gaze into its crystal clear turquoise depths. The water is 20 feet deep here—an ideal swimming and diving area, and breathtakingly beautiful to look at. When we've had our fill, we begin our unique trip through a totally different kind of wilderness. There's an eerie quality to this Florida swampland, with the bulbous trunks of its cypress giants and their goblin knees. The trees, sodden from the recent rains, look black and forbidding on this cloudy day. Even the water looks black. Birds call to us as we paddle silently and effortlessly over the placid, mirror-like surface. We pass into Holmes Creek where the banks are higher, and wildflowers abound. Azaleas, honeysuckle, magnolia, and dogwood can be spotted amid the cedars, maple, gums, pines, and varieties of oaks. The many bayous, small springs, and creeks that feed the main creek offer opportunities to explore. Florida shellcrackers, crappies, and bream invite fisherfolk, and if you look hard enough you can spot otter, raccoons, and turtles. Alligators are rare in these parts. There's lots of bird activity high in the branches overhead—a flash of red as cardinals fly into the bushes, and a lone giant gray heron swoops past our canoe before it disappears between the trees. About halfway through our trip, we enjoy the sight of some elegant estates set back from the bluffs and bordered by colorful azaleas. The Vickers purchased an acre of land at the takeout point, and Harold, big and burly and grinning, is there to meet us and help us disembark. Go with the flow on this one, and you'll have no problem. It's three hours of pure pleasure.

GENERAL RATING: XXX
DIFFICULTY: EASY
SCENERY: EXCELLENT

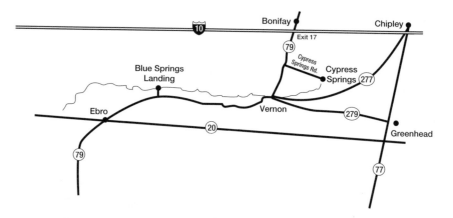

Cypress Springs

CHIPOLA RIVER

The river's head is located in southeastern Alabama, and it flows south some 80 miles or so to the Apalachicola River, disappearing underground at intervals before it becomes navigable just above the SR 152 bridge in the northern section of Jackson County. The Chipola undergoes a variety of changes in color, from a clear emerald green to a deeper green, becoming a muddy yellow during the rainy season. The numerous springs along the run and the dry caves, called "The Ovens," which have been carved into the limestone bluffs by centuries of water action, are an added source of interest to paddlers. The area was once the camping grounds of the Chatot Indians, from whom the river probably got its name after undergoing the usual spelling variations. Nearby is the old Bellamy Plantation site, a pre-Civil War farm indicative of the agriculture that once was the area's livelihood. Paper mills continue to thrive here, but the companies are generous about allowing campers and canoeists to pull up on shore.

CANOE RENTALS

BEAR PAW CANOE TRAILS
P.O. BOX 621
MARIANNA, FL 32446
(904) 482-4948

CHIPOLA OUTDOORS
1312 EAST HIGHWAY 90
MARIANNA, FLORIDA 32446
(904) 482-7343

To find BEAR PAW CANOE TRAILS, take Highway 71 south From I-10; take exit 21 and travel one-half mile. Turn right on Magnolia Road (Hwy. 280), travel one mile, cross the river bridge, and turn right onto the dirt road at the sign (immediately after crossing the bridge). The office is approximately one-quarter mile further. Rickie McAlpin and Anna Harcus, who operate this livery, had some hard luck awhile back when they were flooded out, but they're rebuilding, and by the time this book is in print, they should have complete facilities including restrooms, a general supply store and bait shop, and picnic areas. Canoes rent, at present, for $15 for three- to eight-mile trips; $20 for 15 miles; tubing trips for $4; and a special "Dry Creek" trip for $25. They suggest you bring a flashlight to explore the caverns, plenty of food and cold drinks, litter bags, and bathing suits and towels. They emphasize: No pets, no guns, no littering. The canoes are Coleman.

CONCESSIONS

The Bear Paw store will offer about anything you'll need in the way of canoeing and fishing supplies. The many caves and caverns, and the numerous springs located on this run provide enough interest to make you happy. If you want to explore further, the Florida Caverns State Park is located nearby, offering access to more of the caves.

THE TRAIL

Rickie shuttles us upstream to Spring Creek, which feeds out of Merritts Mill Pond, and from there it's downstream to the Chipola for eight pleasurable miles. As he settles us into our canoe, Rickie tells us that a record-setting shellcracker, a fish similar to a brim,was recently caught in these waters. A rope swing at the launch site indicates that the pure waters here provide an excellent swimming hole. We navigate deftly around a few deadfalls, pass under the railroad trestle, and enter the depths of the forest.

Just when we think there's no way a river can offer us a new experience, we venture into Spring Creek, struck by its singular, pristine beauty, fresh, clear water, and lush vegetation. It's dim and lovely under the heavy canopy of magnificent old cypress trees and ancient

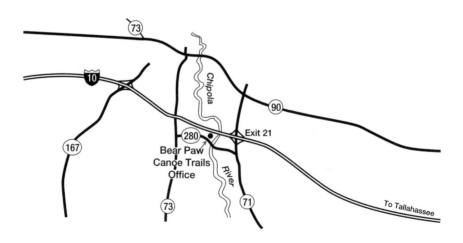

gnarled oaks adorned with wisps of Spanish moss. When we reach the Chipola, the water broadens, and we bear left, continuing on down the "easy river." It's just as scenic here, and wider, with high, heavily wooded bluffs and colorful wildflowers. A great blue heron swoops across our bow, and other unseen birds call to each other in the brush. The current is swifter now, and we float awhile, savoring the stillness and the tangy fresh smells of soil and centuries-old wood. Cypress knees, like remnants of picket fences, line the shore. The hum of traffic on the bridge ahead tells us we've neared the end of our journey . . . a delightful trip, ideal for novice paddlers. Next time, we'll try those caves. Today, after having canoed over 30 miles in two days, we're all paddled out!

GENERAL RATING: XXXX
DIFFICULTY: EASY
SCENERY: EXCELLENT

Chipola River

COLDWATER CREEK

A tributary of the spring-fed Blackwater River, this body of water in Santa Rosa County, in the northwest portion of Florida called the Panhandle, is known to locals as "The BIG COLDWATER." Santa Rosa, with the single largest concentration of superb canoe trails in the state, was designated "The Canoe Capital of Florida" in 1981 by the Florida Legislature. It's a short drive from Mobile, Alabama; Pensacola; Montgomery, Alabama; Fort Walton Beach; and Panama City. Don't let the creek's muddy appearance after a hard rain fool you, because the water is actually about as pure as it gets these days. "Blackwater," which runs through much of Florida, is stained by tannic and organic acids seeping down from the neighboring swamps and pine forests. Like its sister streams, the Blackwater, Sweetwater, and Juniper creeks, the Coldwater originates in southernmost Alabama, bordered on the north by the Conecuh National Forest, where the lack of development or agricultural activity ensures the purity of its water. During fair weather, you can count on it being clear, shallow, and swift with a luminous sandy bottom. The Big Coldwater is the westernmost stream in the Blackwater Forest, and possibly derives its name from the fact that it is also the widest and swiftest. A fact to keep in mind: A time change occurs when you cross the Apalachicola River. If you're coming from the south, you gain an hour; from the north, you lose an hour.

CANOE RENTALS

ADVENTURES UNLIMITED
Route 6, Box 283
Milton, FL 32570
(904) 623-6197 or (904) 626-1669

ACTION ON BLACKWATER
Highway 4, P.O. Box 283
Baker, FL 32531
(904) 537-2997

BOB'S CANOE RENTALS
4569 Plowman Lane
Milton, FL 32570
(904) 623-5457

BLACKWATER CANOE RENTALS
10274 Pond Road
Milton, FL 32583
(904) 626-1669

Because ADVENTURES UNLIMITED, operating in the area since 1976, offers excellent overnight accommodations, we chose this particular livery as headquarters for navigating the splendid waterways of the Black Forest. Take exit 10 from I-75 and turn North on Highway 87. Or, if you're traveling Highway 90 in Milton, turn north on Highway 87. On 87, go 12 miles and watch for the yellow sign on the right. Turn right and continue four miles to ADVENTURES UNLIMITED, Tomahawk Landing. We were quartered in "Magnolia," a rustic but nicely appointed little cabin with a screen porch overlooking a small tributary of Coldwater Creek. The rates for the cabins range from $29 for a "Treehouse"; $39 for air-conditioned camp style; $59 for a one-bedroom cottage with a fireplace and kitchenette, like ours; to a two-bedroom historic cottage that rents for $89. Built in 1901, it was moved to its present location by the Sanborns. It was once the home of "Granny" Peadon, a well-loved and respected member of the nearby community of Springhill in Red Rock.

Group rates for the cabins are also available. There are no phones or TVs in the rooms, and there's no restaurant at present on the premises, so we advise bringing a good supply of food, drinks, and snacks if you plan to stay a few nights. The town of Milton, which has a few good eateries, is about an hour's drive.

Bob Galbraith, genial manager of Adventures Unlimited, informs us that approximately 60,000 tourists visit the 85-acre family-oriented resort each year, lured by the excellent kayaking, canoeing, tubing, paddle-boating, hiking, camping, and social events—like hayrides—it offers. They do have a few basic rules: no pets, no firearms, no jet skis, no alcohol on the rivers. When the Sanborn brothers, Jack and Mike, began their venture twenty years ago, they owned a mere two acres and were open only during the summer months, but today theirs is a year-round business. Specifically, canoes rent for $12 per person for short trips; $13 per person for day trips. Overnight trips are available for the more adventurous. The day trips, four miles to 17 miles, have no hourly time limits, except for the 2 p.m. curfew. This is one of the trips we can recommend for the hot summer months because you can pull up to one of the many inviting and easily accessible sandbars along the way to enjoy picnicking and swimming. Indeed, their big season, Bob tells us, begins on Memorial Day and ends on Labor Day. Our canoe, an Old Town, fashioned from an indestructible hard plastic, proved to be lightweight, quiet, and easier to maneuver than most. Aluminum and fiberglass canoes are also available.

The facility is open daily from 8 a.m. to 5 p.m., except for Christmas Day and Thanksgiving Day. Because of its popularity, it's best to call for reservations even though there are are some 400 canoes on hand, some for sale. One note of caution: Canoes rent only until 2 p.m., and that's a hard-and-fast rule. "We screen our customers as to their ability," Bob says. "We don't want people staying out after dark, and we don't send them out if flood conditions prevail or the current is too swift, or if they can't manage a canoe. To make extra sure, we conduct trail sweeps after hours to make sure everyone has safely returned."

CONCESSIONS

Adventures Unlimited is a destination resort offering quality service to its many visitors. The office is located in a roomy frame structure that also sells supplies, snacks, cold drinks, souvenirs, and contains a deli and snack bar. Clean, modern restrooms and showers are handy. A catering service provides excellent food for large parties. If you want to explore, there are many attractions in the area including those in Pensacola, and the many beautiful state parks, notably Blackwater River State Park, 15 miles northeast of Milton off US 90.

THE TRAIL

Bob shuttles us to The Big Coldwater and guides us to the water's edge, easily carrying the canoe on his shoulders, then helps us embark with our paddles and life jackets. (Cushions will soon be unavailable at all canoe liveries because of new regulations, but until then, if you need one, bring your own.) The creek is a muddy yellow ochre from the recent rains, and somewhat higher than its usual one to six-and-a-half feet, but the opaque color and the swift current don't discourage us.

We've been anxious to try what many consider the best canoeing in Florida. After making sure we navigate safely under the bridge at the outset of our trip, Bob waves us off. The creek is narrow and winding at first, and log jams and other deadfalls mark the way but are easy to circumnavigate. And we find the fast pace and the occasional patches of Florida "whitewater" exhilarating; the many sharp turns provide just enough challenge to make the trip interesting. At times, John, who's in the stern, merely steers the boat as we're propelled by the current. We figure one reason these particular creeks are so popular is the preponderance of large, powder-white sandbars that crop up at almost every bend, offering perfect spots to disembark and have a swim. "Party Island," aptly named, is one of the largest, and the scene of many a barbeque and group picnic, we're told.

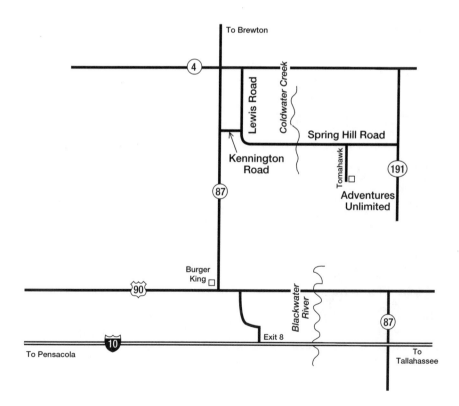

The Panhandle, we find, offers totally unique scenery with its towering cypress trees glistening with new lime-green growth. To add to our enjoyment, wildflowers abound in the heavy foliage: dogwood, honeysuckle, magnolia, azalea in all their brilliant hues, typical of spring in the northern climes. There's even a different breed of turtle—golden brown with dark spots, called soft-shell turtles—along with the usual varieties of snapping turtles.

Near the end of our journey the creek widens, and we float on in, enjoying the silence broken only by the soughing of the wind in the Florida pines, the call of birds, and the ripples of our paddles. Prominent signs mark the way to the takeout where we pull the canoe up on the sandy shore, an easy job. We need only carry our paddles and life jackets back to the office. We have paddled about four hours, electing to take a shorter trip. The entire course is about 17 miles, and takes a few hours longer.

GENERAL RATING: XXX
DIFFICULTY: EASY (IT'S CONSIDERED A "NOVICE RIVER,"
ALTHOUGH SOME BASIC SKILL IS REQUIRED TO AVOID DEADFALLS
AND NAVIGATE SHARP TURNS).
SCENERY: EXCELLENT

Coldwater Creek

BLACKWATER RIVER

The river, located in the Panhandle, is not to be confused with the one bearing the same name in the Everglades. This Blackwater River, like its tributaries, The BIG COLDWATER, SWEETWATER, and JUNIPER CREEK, is fed by seepage springs, and is said to be one of the purest sand-bottom waterways in the world despite its murky appearance. It is darker than the creeks that branch out from it, a fact that no doubt inspired its name; but on closer inspection, it is actually a clear, deep rusty color, rather than black, resulting from a mixture of the tannic elements and red clay that seep into its depths. It is still in a natural state for most of its fifty miles, and its remote, undeveloped acres make canoeing its length a pleasure. Red cedar dominates the hardwoods flourishing on the banks against a background of longleaf pine, wax myrtle, and other mixed hardwoods. We've learned that logging and turpentine industries once flourished in these parts, and you can still see the faint trails leading to the interior, and the railroad trestles that carried the products to their destinations.

Bob shuttles us to the BLACKWATER RIVER STATE PARK to embark on this particular journey. The entrance fee is absorbed by ADVENTURES UNLIMITED, but there's a parking fee of $2.12 if you leave your own vehicle on the grounds. With Bob's help, the launch is effortless, but, once again, he watches our progress to make sure we pass safely between the pilings of the Kennedy Bridge, and skate the partly submerged tree stumps and other debris that block our path. Once underway, it seems we're all alone, skimming the dark surface of the Blackwater.

The shrill cacophony of a multitude of unseen frogs greets us at one bend of the river, a sound like that of static on a shortwave radio. Otherwise, it's still and eerily lonesome in the spring—ideal for us before the onslaught of the tubers and campers. We skirt giant trees lying prone in the water, their stark, silvery skeletons forming patterns of sunken beauty.

About halfway down the river, we're reminded it's a weekend when we encounter canoeists from a nearby livery. Suddenly, we witness a canoe capsizing a few hundred yards up ahead, spilling its occupants.

Panicked, they try to cling to the overturned craft, the young woman screaming that she can't swim. Her male companion flounders helplessly, it seems. With our accumulated wisdom, we shout instructions, telling the girl to hold fast to the life jacket bobbing behind her, and

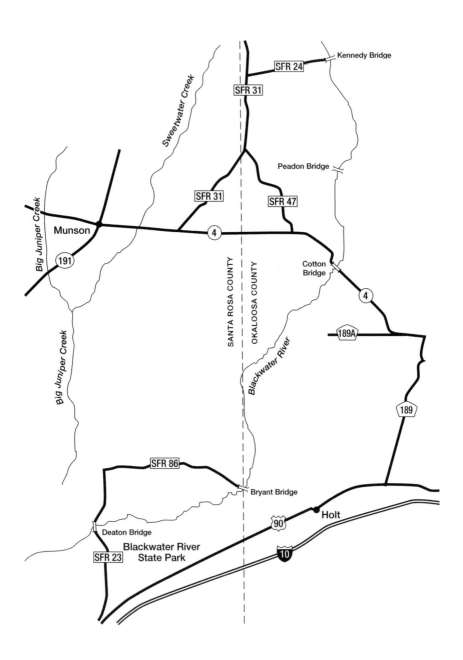

to paddle to shallow water. We advise the young man to push the canoe to shore to right it before we retrieve the paddles and some of the gear that has shot downstream in the swift waters. Battling the upstream current, we return to the unlucky pair. Clinging to branches to keep our own craft in place, we make sure they're safely underway once more before we leave them behind. We're happy to help. After all, we've experienced a similar disaster recently on the Turner River. But the young woman has broken a basic rule: She wasn't wearing a life vest even though she can't swim.

As we near the end of our trip, the number of bathers and people picnicking on the sandbars increases, and there's a distinct smell of woodsmoke and barbecue. The Blackwater River State Park is a haven for campers and hikers. Once we pass beneath the Deaton Bridge, we spot a husky young attendant from Adventures Unlimited waiting on the sandy shore to greet us. He helps us out of the canoe, then hoists it to his broad shoulders, and, finally, lashes it to the top of the van. We've canoed approximately four hours, electing to forego the tail end of the river that's usually heavily congested with boat traffic. It's been an eventful day, and we're ready for a hot shower and a drink afterward on the porch of our little cabin on the creek.

GENERAL RATING: XX
SCENERY: GOOD
DIFFICULTY: EASY TO MODERATE
NOTE: SEE "COLDWATER CREEK" (4) FOR CANOE RENTALS

Blackwater River

JUNIPER CREEK

One of the smaller of the BLACKWATER RIVER tributaries fed by seepage springs, JUNIPER CREEK is usually canoed along with SWEETWATER CREEK, but recent floods have made that impossible at this time. Bob advises us that some canoeists who lack experience have been turned away altogether on this spring day because the Juniper is higher and swifter than usual, indicating an arduous and potentially hazardous trip. We feel flattered he considers us skilled enough to attempt it. We are shuttled by van to the embarkation point where Bob checks the water level. Usually, the creek is shallow and you're able to wade sections of it, but right now it's up, about four feet deep, deeper in places. He decides it's manageable, cautioning us to watch carefully for obstructions in the water and fallen trees that might block our path, and advising us to wear our life vests. He carries the canoe to the water's edge, launches us, and makes sure we paddle safely between the pilings of the bridge.

The Juniper is narrower and more twisting than the Big Coldwater, but similar in nature with its many white sandbars and heavily wooded banks. As we continue, the banks become steeper, and you can see the grooves floodwaters have carved into the red rock bluffs. We've been told the clay from this sandstone can be used for making pottery.

Because the heavy tourist season has yet to begin, there's little sign of life, no sound except for the calling of birds and the chorus of insects and frogs. There's a new vista at each turn—tall pines like rows of sentries, gnarled oaks, red cedar (common to the area), and cypress canopies overhead. Flecks of foam, like white flower petals, loosed by the occasional "rapids," spiral in the current ahead of us. The air smells fresh and woodsy, and there's a fresh breeze fanning us as we paddle effortlessly. It's a trip "to die for!" We welcome the absence of boat traffic and the loudspeakers that accompany party boats. Here, because of the usually shallow water, only small skiffs like bass boats can navigate, and jet skis are firmly denied access to all but the lower, more commercial end of the waterway. There's no worry about "potty-stops" on these trips; there are plenty of low white sandbars where you can shore the canoe without much effort, and stretch your legs. Our pick-up time has been arranged beforehand, and there are easy takeout sites on both sides of the bridge which marks the end of our trip . . . about three hours of sheer pleasure.

GENERAL RATING: XXXX
DIFFICULTY: EASY (MODERATE WHEN WATER IS HIGH AND
CURRENT SWIFT)
SCENERY: MAGNIFICENT TO EXCELLENT

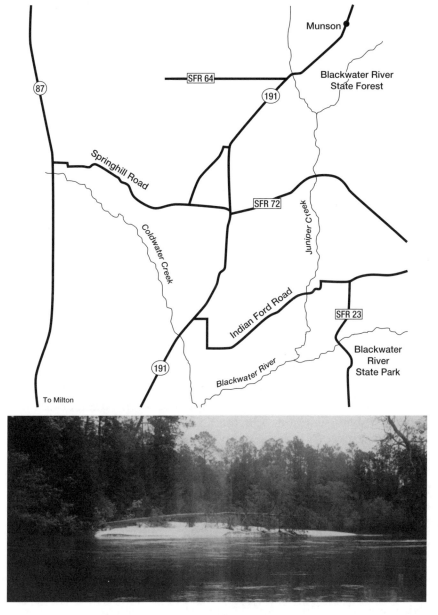

Juniper Creek

ECOFINA RIVER

The river, not to be confused with Econfina Creek, located in Bay and Washington counties, is as unpredictable and challenging as it is beautiful. Unfortunately, Ecofina Creek is not accessible to those who don't have their own canoes, plus it is shallow and almost unnavigable in some sections. The Econfina River in Taylor County, on the other hand, is a clear and unspoiled little stream, surprisingly beautiful, and another of the state's best-kept secrets. Econfina is a Muskogean Indian word meaning "natural bridge," referring, it's said, to the bridge that once existed on the Econfina Creek where SR 20 crosses the stream. There is no trace of it today. A note of interest: The river, 100 miles east of the creek, may bear the same name, but Econfina, in reference to the Creek, is pronounced "fina," as in "finer"; the Econfina River is pronounced "Ee-con-FEE-na."

CANOE RENTALS

ECONFINA ON THE GULF
Econfina River State Park
Rt. 1, Box 255
Lamont, FL 32396
(904) 584-2135

Take Highway 98 from Perry, and head west until you reach SR 14 where you turn south. Continue traveling on this road, noting the signs identifying Econfina On the Gulf, until it dead-ends and you arrive at the river. Not highly publicized, and unknown to us before our trip to the Panhandle—we just happened upon it while searching for the river's whereabouts—the livery operates with a grand total of four canoes in partnership with the Econfina River State Park on the Gulf of Mexico. The canoe rental office is closed on Mondays and Tuesdays, but hours are 6 a.m. to 6 p.m., Wednesday through Saturday and Sundays from 8–7. The office of Econfina On the Gulf is located in a building near the water's edge within a private community of the same name. Canoes rent for a bargain rate of $2 per hour, and this facility is in the process of expanding its services. "We'll go with the demand," the management told us, and added they hoped our book would generate greater interest. You're left pretty much to yourself, getting the canoe off the rack and hauling it to the water's edge, but the attendant assured us they're ready to help those who may not be able to lift and lug. It's another round trip . . . most liveries in these parts don't seem to be interested at this date in shuttle service, but some are contemplating adding it. In spite of its idyllic appearance, the river is another breeding ground for "no-seeums." They're ferocious here, so be generous with the repellent.

CONCESSIONS

Econfina On the Gulf is a destination resort noted for its excellent fishing, and attracts regular customers as far away as Georgia and North and South Carolina. Redfish, trout, brim, and bass abound. There's a charming restaurant, a conference center with complete kitchen facilities, and a general store on the premises, and fishing guides and boats are available along with bait and tackle. Accommodations include villas, apartments, motel rooms, RV parking, and tent and trailer camping. Rates are $85 overnight for a condo, $45 per night for a motel room. Camping fees at the adjacent ECONFINA STATE PARK, which maintains the grounds and is responsible for the lack of litter and the pristine quality of the river, are $14 per night for two, and primitive camping costs $6 per night. There are picnic tables on the grounds, and a bathhouse with clean restrooms. Rustic hiking and equestrian trails are also available.

THE TRAIL

When spring returns to the Big Bend, as they call this section of Florida, it brings ideal temperatures for canoeing, longer days and light winds, and a time when "fishing really kicks off." It's the season for dogwood, azalea, and magnolia blossoms. Awed by the beauty of the river, we bear left at the onset of the trip, enjoying the rustic homes on stilts along the way, half-hidden by the heavy foliage. We pass the condos of the little community, and a few moments later, we enter the wilderness we crave. It's the north Florida Gulf Coast where rivers meet the sea, and tidal marshes flourish as the water shifts from fresh to saline. Local environmentalists and commercial fisherfolk are conducting a battle to preserve the wetlands and the natural ecosystem. Here, the river seems to be oblivious of its possible fate, narrow and winding, placid and easy to paddle. The shoreline looms close with countless cypress, Florida pines, and palms rising from the tropical undergrowth. We spot an eagle's nest high in the branches of a dead cypress, and just as we aim our camera, an eagle rises and soars out of sight. Unwilling to miss any part of this wild and scenic river, we head back in the other direction to explore the segment that culminates, eventually, in the Gulf of Mexico. The river is wider here, the shore uninhabited, and except for an occasional fisherman, we see no sign of humans. We've been told there's very little boat traffic except at the point where the river actually meets the Gulf, and the fishing is exceptionally good.

From pine flatlands to oak and palm hammocks, to broad expanses of salt marsh dotted with pine islands, Ecofina State Park, with its 3,377 acres, offers spectacular vistas. Several osprey nests are visible from the canoe, and one contains the elegant bird and its offspring. Root formations at the water's edge form beautiful, intricate patterns, and each bend of the river offers a new and breathtaking view. A sudden, heavy downpour curtails our trip, but thanks to our rain gear, and the waterproof Pelican case my son, Dan Callahan, sent us after learning of our mishap on the Turner River, we're able to keep the camera and ourselves dry. It's pleasant paddling in the rain, and we return to the headquarters pleased to have discovered yet another hideaway bargain river. The entire round trip to the Gulf, we're told, would have taken us approximately three hours.

GENERAL RATING: XXXX
DIFFICULTY: EASY
SCENERY: EXCELLENT
ANOTHER PAMPERED PADDLER'S PLUS!

Econfina River

PART II

NORTHERN PENINSULA

ALAFIA RIVER

L ocated in southern Hillsborough County, the river runs from Keysville Bridge to Alderman's Ford County Park. The navigable upper section of the river is located about an hour east of Tampa on State Road 640 off Highway 60, with none of the city's industrial skyline in sight. From the SR 39 exit on I-4 in Plant City, travel south on SR 39 for 12 miles to Alderman's Ford County Park on the left. You can also take I-75 and exit south of Tampa on Highway 60. Go approximately one-half mile south past the Alafia River bridge and turn west on Thompson Road (right).

Alafia (pronounced "AL-uh-fye" by the Seminoles) is a Seminole Indian name meaning "hunting ground," descriptive of the abundance of deer and wild turkey once found in the area. Centuries ago, the first settlers sharing the territory of these Native Americans changed the spelling to Alfiers, then began to call their community Sapling Woods. Through the years, the name was changed again to "Elfers," which more closely resembled the original spelling. During the Seminole Indian Wars in the mid-1800s, some skirmishes took place in the vicinity. Because it was a favorite Indian hunting ground, some well-informed paddlers still manage to find artifacts. Sharks' teeth can be gathered in the shoals even by novices.

CANOE RENTALS

ALAFIA CANOE RENTALS, INC.
4419 River Drive
Valrico, FL 33594
(813) 689-8645

CANOE HEAVEN
Route 1, Box 414J
Valrico, FL 33594
(813) 689-2017

ALAFIA RIVER CANOE OUTPOST
4712 Lithia Pinecrest Road
Valrico, FL 33594
(813) 681-2666

All rental services are excellent. But because it's a popular river, advance reservations are advised, and weekdays are best. We chose ALAFIA RIVER CANOE RENTALS, open daily from February 15th to September 15th, 8 a.m. to 7 p.m., except on Thursdays and unsafe high-water-level days. Call in advance to avoid disappointment. The owners and managers, Sybil and Bob Cribbs, advertise that it's the oldest and largest livery on the river. The $25 fee for an all-day canoe trip includes paddles, cushions, and life jackets. A shuttle takes you upstream, and you paddle down river; pickup times at the downstream takeout point are prearranged. Overnight camping gear can be obtained for those who like to rough it. The friendly concessionaires welcome first-timers and offer a few brief instructions. You're given detailed maps of the river, which allow you to determine whether you'd like a half-day or a full-day trip, or one that involves only a few hours of paddling. A 12-mile trip, which takes approximately 4 hours, is the most popular. Vans leave for the launch weekdays on the hour from 8 a.m. until 1 p.m.; summers, weekends, holidays, every 30 minutes until 2 p.m. Restrooms and showers are handy. We bring a swimsuit and a towel if it's a warm day, and a towel and a change of clothes on any day!

CONCESSIONS

You can purchase supplies, snacks, hats, and T-shirts at the rental buildings of both canoe outposts. The river passes through two county parks: Alderman's Ford and Lithia Springs. Lithia Springs has swimming, restrooms, shower facilities, and camping. Alderman's Ford provides the same services plus nature trails for hiking, horseback riding, or biking.

THE TRAIL

The mystique of the Alafia River keeps hundreds of people coming back year after year, thus you're liable to run into crowds on weekends, especially in the summer. But on weekdays you can usually find the quiet you seek. ALAFIA CANOE RENTALS launches its customers at Alderman's Ford. There, Bob carries the canoe on his broad shoulders, which is the way we like it. As we happily start out, his cheerful parting words are, "If you don't get back today, we'll tell tomorrow's people to look for you." It seems we're all alone on the narrow, twisting trail that meanders through a gnarled upland forest, sharing its beauty with wading birds, grazing cattle, otters, turtles, and an occasional sleepy, bored-looking alligator. It's said that Florida panthers and bobcats lurk somewhere in the heavy forest. We did spot a deer and a wild boar. A chicken hawk stares down at us from a tall pine. Happily, there's no sign of the Tampa skyline.

The river flows swiftly over a limestone bed that exposes shoals in low water and gives you the exhilarating illusion that you're navigating whitewater. It does take a little extra skill to maneuver a canoe on these "rapids," and you're reminded of the Indians who once passed over the very same spot, and the Spanish explorers who followed in their wake. We like to sit on the shoals on a warm day to enjoy the cool, rushing water on our legs while we sift through the shells for fossils and sharks' teeth. Each time we round a bend there's a new scenic delight as we breathe in the wonderful aromas of pines, oaks, and cedars. Our sleek, silver craft cuts through the swift current (with the flow, of course), and when we feel hunger pangs, we beach the canoe on a strip of white sand to enjoy our picnic lunch. We stop often just to prolong the trip, losing all track of time before we spot our journey's end, and reluctantly leave the Florida wilderness behind.

GENERAL RATING: XXXX
DIFFICULTY: MODERATE
SCENERY: EXCELLENT

Alafia River

BARTRAM CANOE TRAIL
(DURBIN CREEK TO JULINGTON CREEK)

St. Johns County in the central peninsula is home to countless small hidden streams and creeks which are a delight to explore. Durbin Creek, a slow-moving freshwater stream, flows to the more prominent St. Johns River, and is located within easy reach of Jacksonville and the beaches of the Atlantic Coast. The popular section of the creek is known as the Bartram Canoe Trail, named after William Bartram, the famous naturalist who wrote of his travels and discoveries throughout this wilderness section of Florida.

CANOE RENTALS

OUTDOOR ADVENTURES
6110-7 Powers Ave.
Jacksonville, FL 32217
(904) 739-1960

Howard Solomon, a former practicing attorney in Jacksonville, decided he preferred the freedom of outdoor life to the daily grind of court procedure. His OUTDOOR ADVENTURES is apparently the only organized enterprise for canoe rentals covering the vast area of water trails in this remote section of the state. Solomon customizes trips according to your interests and ability. Since these excursions involve traveling some distance to various embarkation points, you need to call one week in advance and send a 50% deposit. Balance is payable on departure. Solomon accepts major credit cards and local checks with ID. Young and engaging, his vitality and boundless enthusiasm make the lengthy trips to the embarkation points pleasurable and informative. The rendezvous spot is usually in the Publix parking lot on the corner of San Jose Boulevard (SR 13) and Orange Pickers Road in Jacksonville County. He'll give you more detailed instructions when you call.

The sturdy, steady Old Town-Discovery canoes, our personal favorites with their comfortable contoured seats, rent for $45 for a self-guided trip including transportation to put-in, which is always our preference. Guided trips cost $35 per person, $65 per pair. Fees seem a little steep until you figure that the driving time in Solomon's van to the departure point often takes an hour-and-a-half, and sometimes adds up to as much as a hundred miles round trip, which includes delivery and pickup. (You can check with him personally if it's more convenient to meet him at the waterway of your choice). His guided trips (6-person minimum) include round-trip transportation from the rendezvous site, beverages, and lunch, and at least one on water interpretive guide. Solomon also rents kayaks; provides certified canoe or kayak instruction; arranges bicycling, backpacking, and hiking tours; plans overnight trips complete with meals; and offers river cruising. Solomon's prearranged paddling destination trips include: Cumberland Island (a saltwater paddle); Okefenokee Swamp; Suwannee River; St. Marys River; Ichetucknee Springs; Silver River; St. Johns River; Durbin Creek; McGirt's Creek; and Black Creek. He'll even take you as far as Big Shoals on the Suwannee north of High Springs, a whitewater trip which necessitates some portage and tricky maneuvering, for the more experienced canoeists. If you're feeling particularly adventurous, try one of his hot-air balloon flights!

CONCESSIONS

Thanks to Solomon's concern, we were able to set up headquarters at THE TOCOI FISH CAMP, a riverfront hideaway in Tocoi, a dot on the map located at the mouth of Tocoi Creek on the St. Johns River on Highway 13. The kind proprietors provided us with a fully furnished apartment with a separate living room and bedroom, a full kitchen, and a private deck overlooking the water and the sunsets. The facilities include covered boat slips, a boat ramp, and a general store and bait shop next door with a rustic but tidy little luncheonette providing reasonably priced breakfasts and lunches. The exposed rafters, the wide porch overlooking the water, and the small tables lend a homey atmosphere, and the service is quick and friendly. Lodging rates (per double occupancy) are $85 in season (Feb. 1 to Sept. 31); $65 off season (Oct. 1 to Jan. 31). Don't count on a place nearby to dine, but if you don't mind driving between six and ten miles farther down Highway 13, there are a couple of quaint seafood places (both closed on Mondays) on the water. The managers at Tocoi will give you directions. We elected to keep our own snacks in the handy refrigerator, and had our glass of wine and a light supper at the table in our room overlooking the water. The proprietors inform us they are contemplating the purchase of a few canoes to paddle a scenic 45-minute little route called Tocoi Creek, and by the time this book goes to print, they might be available.

There are so many attractions in the Jacksonville/St. Augustine area it would be impossible to list them all, but one that deserves special mention is THE HUGENOT MEMORIAL BEACH PARK, on Highway A1A at the Fort George Inlet on the southeast side of the bridge five miles west of Jacksonville. With the Atlantic Ocean on the east, Fort George Inlet on the north, and St. Johns River on the south, it has everything, including the U.S. Navy docks, home of the Mayport Naval Fleet, an impressive sight.

THE TRAIL

We meet Solomon at Publix, as arranged (the self-guided trips on this particular waterway usually originate at Clark's Boat Ramp in Trader's Hill), and follow him in our own van to the launch site, about ten miles away, where he helps us embark. We begin our paddle in an enchanted, swampy setting where the creek is narrow and the trees create a shady canopy. But its remote beauty has made us forget that this is a haven for all kinds of vicious, stinging insects. In spite of our precautions, our repellent doesn't prevent me from sustaining numerous bites which leave large welts, the result of attacks by yellow flies. I get no sympathy. "It's part of living on the river," we're told. The next day, the swelling increases, and has to be dosed with Benadryl and cold compresses. In the future, I'll wear long-sleeved shirts and jeans for this kind of trip. My discomfort is forgotten for the time being as we pass by ancient cypress trees reminiscent of Florida's early logging days, and the remains of old bridge pilings on what was once the road from St. Augustine to Jacksonville. A lone osprey is flushed from the undergrowth as we glide by, and perches high in a tree watching our progress. We spot wood ducks and herons and other familiar wading birds. We're told alligators like these dark, tannin-stained waters, and that lucky, observant paddlers can identify eagles, wild turkeys and boars, and whitetail deer.

Once we reach the wider, more commercial expanse of Julington Creek, the idyllic portion of our journey is over. We encounter power boats and noisome jet skis, which preclude further wildlife sightings, but we try to focus on the truly beautiful lily pad gardens, alive with purple and gold blossoms, and the heavily wooded shoreline. You need cool, protective clothing for this trip, lots of sunscreen, strong insect repellent, and a hat. As we near our destination, a hawk soars overhead and disappears amid the trees, and musical croaking sounds from deep within the lily pads accompany our last few hundred yards. We pull our canoe up on the banks, overturn it, and leave the gear underneath, as instructed. Clark's Fish Camp, heralded as "The People's Choice," is a popular seafood and drinking establishment located on the long wooden pier there, but, to our disappointment, it's also closed on Mondays. We head to our car and drive back to the Tocoi Fish Camp and our inviting lodgings.

GENERAL RATING: XXX
DIFFICULTY: EASY
SCENERY: EXCELLENT ON THE DURBIN CREEK PORTION

Durbin Creek

ST. MARYS RIVER

....

L ike the Suwannee, St. Marys River originates in the dark reflec-
tive waters of the Okefenokee Swamp. It forms the Florida/
Georgia border for a time, flowing steadily for 125 miles toward the
Atlantic Ocean near Fernandina Beach just south of Cumberland
Island. Its name, as in the case of the St. Johns and St. Marks rivers,
for instance, originated with the Catholic Spaniards, who often relied
on the saints mentioned in their Bibles to identify their discoveries.

Isolated and pristine, a lengthy section of this wondrous blackwater river has been designated "Wild and Scenic" by the National Park
Service, and has an interesting history. Old sailing vessels, called
"tramps" by the locals, traveled hundreds of miles to the legendary
St. Marys River to refill their water barrels with the tea-colored but
pure water. Trader's Mill, our destination, was once a thriving trad-
ing post where river boats came to deliver supplies. Some of the
wooden pilings from the docks remain imbedded in the swampy
ground, reminders of the early days of exploration. Before the turn
of the century, places such as White Springs and Suwannee Springs
were health spas where eager visitors from all over the country came
to eat the mullet and bathe in the famed mineral waters.

THE TRAIL

Once again, our guide, Solomon, meets us at Publix, and we start
out on the lengthy but scenic drive to Thompkins Landing in Nassau
County, our embarkation point, the final segment of the river and
considered best for canoeing. "This section is sometimes called 'The
First Coast' because so much of early Florida history took place
here," Solomon explains. "The St. Marys is one of the crookedest
rivers in America," he continues. "It's actually been tracked, a big
horseshoe, constantly curving. It's one of Florida's lesser-known
waterways, but one of the best for canoeists." We agree it's one of
the most breathtaking excursions we've encountered as we paddle
into an ever-changing wonderland of high bluffs, limestone outcroppings, snowy sandbars, and canopied swamps. The water is typically
coffee-colored, but fresh and pure. Toppled trees with their tangled
branches form intricate patterns across the water. It's silent and

beautifully lonely here with an almost total absence of boat traffic and only the call of birds to keep us company. Even the rasp of insects is muted.

Maneuvering between the many easily visible sandbars and dead-falls, and navigating the occasional sharp turns creates just enough challenges to remind us we're in a canoe. A pair of blue herons take flight as if to guide us down the river, and a gator leaves a trail of bubbles as his dark form passes under water just inches away from our canoe. Stands of native Florida trees—cypress, gum, tupelo, live oak, willow, poplar, yellow pine, and river birch—crowd together to form endless varieties of greenery and complex root patterns. Wildlife in the area includes deer, otter, beaver . . . we see their toothmarks everywhere . . . and raccoons. A sudden splash at the river's edge catches us with paddles in midair as an alligator lunges toward a blue heron perched on a log. He sinks quickly below the water as his prey soars safely out of sight.

St. Marys River

There are plenty of inviting sandbars along the way for picnics or potty-stops, and we disembark often to prolong the trip, to take pictures, snack, and stretch our legs. A wide expanse of beach with some rickety tables and the remains of a campfire identifies one of the more popular stopovers. The St. Marys is an excellent touring river, well suited to paddlers of all levels, since development along the banks is scattered and access to the river is limited. It takes three hours to cover the eight-mile trip, but all too soon we're at Trader's Hill on the Georgia side of the river. The fish camp has a boat ramp, picnic tables, restrooms, and campsites at the end of a paved road that turns off Georgia SR 121, a few miles south of Folkston. Solomon is waiting for us as we pull the canoe up on shore. We allow him to carry it to his van, hoist it, and secure it. We watch, admiring his strength. He's far younger than we are, and we're here to be pampered, after all!

GENERAL RATING: XXXX
DIFFICULTY: EASY
SCENERY: SPECTACULAR
A PAMPERED PADDLER'S PLUS!

St. Marys River

McGirt's Creek

....

This is a crooked, little-known waterway, one of Solomon's own discoveries, he claims. It was named after Daniel McGirt, one of Florida's most notorious badmen, whose legendary amassed fortune has never been found. Born in 1750, McGirt grew up in St. Augustine, and was once a patriot soldier with the Georgia Mounted Volunteers, fighting against the British. After an altercation with a superior officer who coveted his horse, he deserted and joined the East Florida Rangers, who were on the side of the British. A lifetime of engaging in robberies and raids ended in his capture and imprisonment, but his exact fate is still in question. It is documented that McGirt owned a farm in 1780, about a mile above the junction of the Ortega and St. Johns rivers, where he and his gang often withdrew between forays. McGirt's Ferry was owned and operated by members of his family, and was used by both forces during the Revolutionary War.

THE TRAIL

"McGirt's Creek is right in the middle of suburbia, and no one knows about it," Solomon says as we take the Blanding Exit off US 295. He's right. This is the kind of hideaway trail we especially love to explore. McGirt's starts north of Jacksonville as a small trickle, and eventually empties into the Ortega River, named after the famous Spanish explorer. With the roar of highway traffic in our ears, we set out, paddle underneath the overpasses, and, a few minutes later, feel as if we've been swallowed up by the silent Florida swamp. It's a narrow, canopied, crooked little stream whose still, dark waters reflect towering bearded oaks and a jungle of giant cypress trees and other hardwoods with their tangled vines. A woodpecker taps out a message accompanied by a chorus of birdcalls deep in the underbrush, sounds that are heard only in still surroundings like these. We imagine the turbaned Timucuan Indians, who occupied this territory before the onset of the Spanish explorers, paddling these same waters, and talk in whispers of wild Dan McGirt and his family and his scruffy outlaw band hunting and fishing here in the wilderness. It's a novice paddle . . . an easy three hours covering six to seven miles of backwoods beauty. Solomon is waiting for us at the site of the Seminole Canoe and Kayak Club, which allows him the use of their wooden dock.

GENERAL RATING: XXXX
DIFFICULTY: EASY
SCENERY: EXCELLENT
ANOTHER PAMPERED PADDLER'S PLUS!

McGirt's Creek

CHASSAHOWITZKA RIVER

To find the river, located in Chassahowitzka, a small settlement south of Homosassa Springs in Citrus County, take Highway 19 South in Homosassa to Route 480. Make a right on Route 480 for approximately 1.5 miles. The name appears almost Russian in its spelling, and locals jokingly refer to it as "Case-o-whiskey." Legendary gangster Al Capone once owned a home on the Chassahowitzka River during the Great Depression years of the '30s, and his presence opened up a great many questionable but profitable job opportunities for the more needy and the more daring. With its heavy tropical underbrush and many hidden bayous, the river was ideal for bootlegging and "rum running." Its exotic name is actually a Seminole Indian term meaning "hanging pumpkin." When the Seminoles migrated to Florida, they discovered an unusual species of pumpkin favored by the ancient Timucuan Indians.

Unlike the usual golden gourds that trail across the ground, this particular plant had apparently been cultivated by the tribe to wind its way some 30 to 40 feet up a tree to dangle its huge globular fruit in the air. Although it does poorly in the wild on its own, it is occasionally seen in the area, and its presence may indicate a site once inhabited by pioneer settlers or Native Americans. It is still grown by the Seminoles of South Florida.

CANOE RENTALS

CHASSAHOWITZKA RIVER LODGE AND CAMPGROUND
8501 W. Miss Maggie Drive
Chassahowitzka, FL 34448
(352) 382-2081

The lodge is a family camp, established in 1929 and run by the county, and is well-equipped to serve the area's recreational needs. Situated nearby under large oak trees, Don's Bait Shop is one of those rustic, picturesque liveries that suits these parts. Don and Looty Millman, the accommodating managers who run the shop independently of the lodge, help you tote an aluminum canoe a few feet down to the ramp, steady it while you climb in, then send you on your way. Canoe rental is reasonable at $10 a day, $6 for a half-day, and includes paddles and cushions. There are also a few canoes to rent for $12 per day next door at the lodge, which offers more modern amenities, but they are offered only to those who camp there.

CONCESSIONS

Don's Bait Shop offers the usual selection of live or frozen shrimp, ice, tackle, and other supplies. There are also cold drinks, beer, and snacks available, but bring your own lunch if you're fussy, or have a bite at Jim and Bob's, a small dining area next door. Don and Looty have a pleasant wooden deck overlooking the water, with tables and chairs where you can socialize and have a drink before you set out, or when you return. The restroom is located in the laundry building out in back, and there's even a shower for those who aren't too discriminating. The lodge has a modern bathhouse, laundry facilities, a pay phone, a fully stocked store, air-conditioned efficiency cabins, a trailer park, an RV park, boats, and a ramp. Guide service is for the use of its patrons only. Nightly sites are rented for a hook-up fee of $16. There's plenty of après-canoeing fun at nearby Weeki-Wachee (which means "small spring") (listing 26) or Homosassa ("some peppers there") Springs (listing 17).

THE TRAIL

The rule of thumb on this trip, which we find out the hard way, is to stay clear of the channel markers to avoid being run down by the many power boats. Even though we ventured out on a weekday, there's plenty of traffic to make us wary. One boat passes within inches of our fragile craft and sends us rocking in its wake. Apparently, because of the shallow river's rocky bottom, there's only one clearly defined route for power boats, and they make sure they let you know about it! But nothing can spoil our first sight of the wide river. Once we get past the little river cottages and on out through the channel, cheered on by a corps of roosting pelicans and anhingas, the scenery is splendid. Like other rivers in the vicinity, the Chassahowitzka is spring-fed and clear with a labyrinth of tidal creeks signaling its emergence into the Gulf of Mexico. The shoreline is laced with mangroves, cedars, sabal palms, cypress, and oak trees. Most of the river is part of the Chassahowitzka National Wildlife Refuge. There are no roads or developments along its scenic six-mile length as it flows through desolate rainforests, only the picturesque ruins of several long-abandoned fish shacks dot the shore.

Because of this, the area is remarkably free of litter. Fish thrive on the rocky bottom, the marsh grass, and other surface vegetation, and we've been told that fishing for largemouth bass, as well as mangrove snapper and trout, is good year-round. The many fisherfolk we encounter attest to the quality of the sport in these waters. We paddle close to shore to check out some of the springs along the way, enjoying the water's clarity and beauty. About halfway, a stiff headwind causes us to paddle more vigorously . . . just enough action to exercise the midsection a bit. After a couple of hours, we pull up to shore to picnic and watch fishermen casting their nets from their flat-bottomed boat. On our return trip, paddling against an almost non-existent current, we turn into several of the inviting little bayous and canopied creeks that, possibly, were once havens for moonshiners. There's no traffic here, only the big wading birds staring at us, unafraid as we glide past, playful otters bobbing near shore, and the constant call of anhingas and cormorants. Allow yourself time to explore some of these charming sidetrips. This river has been largely overlooked, possibly because of the busy boat traffic, but because of its unspoiled wilderness splendor and the many springs that bubble up near shore, it's a worthwhile excursion.

GENERAL RATING: XXX
DIFFICULTY: EASY (MODERATE
WHEN WATER IS HIGH AND
CURRENT SWIFT).
SCENERY: GOOD

Chassahowitzka River

ECONLOCKHATCHEE RIVER

Locals have dubbed this gem of a river that originates in the Econ-lockhatchee Swamp and winds through Orange and Seminole counties, about 13 miles east of Orlando, The Big Econ, but its full name, woven together with words from Creek and Seminole Indians, is far more appropriate. "Ekana," we learn, means "earth; "laika is the word for "mounds" (Indian burial mounds common to the south); "hatchee" is a generic term for "town" or "river"; thus the literal, combined translation: "river of mounds." It is a primitive rain-fed stream that curls through ancient hardwood and cypress forests, and oakpalm hammocks. Local lore has it that luminous lights, known as "Oviedo Lights," can be spotted on certain nights from the CR 419 bridge. Native Americans used the fresh water for drinking and cooking, and as a popular passage for their dugouts to hunt and fish. The river flows northeasterly to its junction with the St. Johns River, where the trail ends one-and-a-half miles downstream (north) of the confluence. Fortunately, the county and the state are doing a good job of buying up land abutting the river to preserve it. Officials and locals alike are currently fighting a proposal for the development of a subdivision on its banks.

CANOE RENTALS

HIDDEN RIVER PARK
15295 E. Colonial Drive
Orlando, FL 32826
(407) 568-5346

From Orlando, take Colonial Drive east (SR 50) and continue for approximately 13 miles to the Hidden River Park canoe sign. This livery, operated from an RV park for the past 21 years, is owned and managed by the Hastings brothers, and seems to be the lone access for the lowly recreational canoeist to one of Florida's most exciting rivers. Several launching sites exist for those who own canoes. Don

Hastings, an affable young man who loves his job, explains that traffic on the river is sparse even during the season. Don and his brother, Ron, are on the job daily, and rates for a canoe or kayak for exploring or fishing at your leisure are: $6, first hour; $3 each additional hour; $15 for 4 or more hours. Two trips are available. Hidden River Park to a launch site about 9 miles downstream where you're picked up at its conclusion takes approximately 3–5 hours, and the river is not always passable there. The cost is $25 per canoe. The alternative trip from Highway 419 to the Snowhill Road Bridge is a 10-mile trip that takes 4–5 hours. You are shuttled to your launch site and picked up at your destination at a pre-arranged time. Don warns that neither excursion is available during dry seasons, and this is one of the facilities that encourages you to phone ahead of time to check what the water levels are. The canoes are aluminum and lightweight should you be forced to engage in a portage or pullover. Be sure to wear boots or suitable old sneakers for this river. Life jackets and comfortable cushions are provided.

CONCESSIONS

Don't expect much in the way of amenities here. There is no concession stand, so bring your lunch, or you can pick up snacks at the nearby convenience store. The restrooms do have running water, and hot showers are available. The Little-Big Econ Park, which you pass on the river, offers hiking trails and picnic tables.

THE TRAIL

If you want a "wild and scenic river," a place to get away from the crowds, the Econlockhatchee is the one for you. It's one of the best kept secrets in the canoe world. Not willing to face possible portages that might be necessary on the more difficult portion of the river, we chose to be shuttled to a launching site about 10 miles upstream for the Highway 419/Snowhill Road Bridge trip. A steep hill leads to the take-out spot, but Don deftly hoists the canoe onto his back and picks his way downward. He's young and able, but you can at least offer to help carry the gear. The river is one of the "blackwater" rivers, stained to the usual deep brown.

Readers should be advised that the onset of this trip is not for the faint-hearted or inexperienced. It's narrow and overgrown, so be prepared for pullovers and log jams. The current is a little swifter than most and requires some tricky navigating, but it's worth the extra effort. This is a chance to test our acquired paddling skills as we encounter hairpin turns, cypress knees, and occasional tangled floating masses of branches and other debris. At one point, we're forced to lean back and flatten ourselves over the seats to skim under a partly submerged tree trunk. The river, with its high, sandy banks presents numerous, inviting, snowy white sandbars for picnics or rest stops. Because the towering trees provide ample shade, it's one of the few trips we recommend for warmer weather. The corkscrew bends of the Econlockhatchee reveal breathtaking views, one delightful surprise after the other. We see our first sign of life after about an hour's paddling when we encounter a fisherman with his young son. The boy proudly hauls up his stringer, heavily laden with bass, bluegill, and catfish. About two hours into our trip, the river widens for the first time, presenting a broad, placid expanse, and we straighten up at last, floating along for a while to rest our backs before it closes in on us again. As we round a bend, we surprise an enormous alligator snooz-

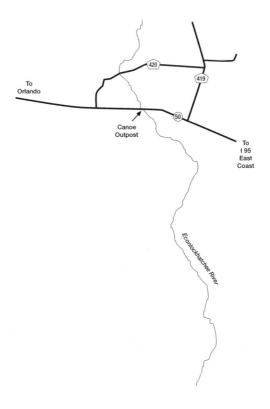

ing in the mud, which heaves itself into the water at our approach with a mighty "that-to-you" splash of its tail before it disappears. We watch the bubbles signaling its progress, and as its huge head emerges once more, it fixes us with one baleful eye before sinking back out of sight. We're back to dodging various deadfalls and fully enjoying it until we arrive at the suspension bridge which we're told is an hour from our takeout spot. Here we stretch our legs and walk across the swaying planks that span a wide section of the river. We're told it was once a railroad trestle for trains that transported cattle and citrus from Sanford on south. Some of the hikers and campers converge at this popular spot, but there are no other signs of life until we reach the concrete Snowhill Road Bridge that signals the end of our excursion. Even after four-and-a-half hours of vigorous paddling, more difficult than any we've encountered until now, we're sorry to see Don waiting on shore to haul up the canoe. We feel great! Although there's a great deal of foliage and broken branches in the canoe, evidence of our our encounters with the capricious "river of mounds," we've conquered it without so much as a scratch.

GENERAL RATING: XXXX
DIFFICULTY: STRENUOUS
SCENERY: SPECTACULAR

Econlockhatchee River *(Photo courtesy of Alan Hastings, Hidden River Park)*

HILLSBOROUGH RIVER

This river is located in Pasco and Hillsborough counties, east of Tampa. Take exit 54 off I-75, then go east on Fowler (SR 582) one-half mile to 9335 E. Fowler Avenue in Thonotosassa. The Hillsborough, one of the most picturesque waterways in the area and a favorite of ours, furnishes about 75% of Tampa's drinking water. It was originally called the "Lockcha-popka-chiska"—"river where one crosses to eat acorns." Seminole Indians were known for their prosaic references. The Spanish called it "the River of Julian de Arriaga." British settlers won out when they renamed it for Will Hills, the Earl of Hillsborough, a Colonial Secretary in the 1700s who was responsible for Great Britain's former control over the Tampa Bay area. The 2,994 acres of the Hillsborough River State Park, one of the earliest in the state, were developed and lovingly preserved by the Civilian Conservation Corps in 1936. Originating in the Green Swamp area of Pasco and Polk counties, the river has five main tributaries: Blackwater Creek, Flint Creek, New River, Trout Creek, and Cypress Creek.

CANOE RENTALS

HILLSBOROUGH RIVER STATE PARK
15402 US 301
North Thonotosassa, FL 33592
(941) 986-1020

Take I-75 to Fowler Avenue (Exit 54). Go east on Fowler (SR 582). Turn northwest on Highway 301, and travel nine miles to the park. The park entrance fee varies. The concessionaire at the water's edge provides canoes for $4 an hour with a $10 deposit or confirmation of your Florida Driver's License. A smiling attendant holds the craft steady while you embark at the dock below, a maneuver that always challenges your sense of balance and involves some judicious weight distribution. The designated nine miles can be covered all or in part. Because we were on a tight schedule, we decided on a 4-hour trip which included the return leg and covered approximately 6 miles. Florida state parks are open from 8 a.m. until sundown, and they're adamant about it. The other rental service providing canoe trips is:

CANOE ESCAPE, INC.

9335 East Fowler Avenue
Thonotosassa, FL 33592
(941) 986-2067

Joe and Jean Faulk, who have been operating their Canoe Escape facility for 15 years, offer a more personalized and equally pleasant river excursion, plus a senior citizen discount. The six varied trips include Sargeant Park to Morris Bridge Park. Two hours paddling time will cover Flint Creek and scenic wilderness; Morris Bridge Park to Trout Creek Park involves a different 4-mile trip; Trout Creek Park to Rotary Park covers 5 miles in 2 hours and explores the river as it widens and passes through Lettuce Lake; trips 4, 5, and 6 combine two or three of the trips to extend your pleasure by as many hours as you wish; Crystal Springs Park to Highway 301 is an all-day trip with about 3 hours of steady paddling and plenty of leisure time to picnic and swim. Canoes rent for $24 for the shorter trips, $28 and $30 for the longer ones. The livery is open weekdays from 9 a.m. to 5 p.m.; weekends, 8–6. Closed Thanksgiving, Christmas Eve, and Christmas Day. Reservations are advised, in which case a deposit is required. In order to preserve the nature experience, the owners do not allow dogs, radios, styrofoam, firearms, or glass.

CONCESSIONS

The Faulks offer soft drinks, ice, snacks, tackle, supplies, and clean restrooms. A concession stand in the main picnic area in the park sells similar supplies. Picnic tables are scattered throughout the park, and there are clean restrooms and public telephones. You can visit legendary Fort Foster where a bloody battle was once fought with the Seminoles, walk the beautiful nature trails, or have a refreshing swim in the man-made swimming pool. Swimming isn't permitted in the river. And leave your booze behind. It's against park regulations.

THE TRAIL

Because of the lack of strong currents, it's fairly easy paddling, both going and returning. The beautiful, scenic Hillsborough flows over rock outcrops of Suwanee limestone, creating small sets of mini-rapids, which is about all the "whitewater" the occasional canoeist cares to handle, and provides some low-key excitement. The jungly, winding path takes us through swamps and hammocks dominated by the usual varieties of Florida wading birds, turtles, and snakes. The vegetation-choked waters, stained to a murky brown by the tannic and humic acids, are a haven for alligators. We spot a 10-foot reptile before it sinks out of sight at the first ripple of our oars. Wondering how many others lurk beneath us, we glide past at a respectable distance under the apple-green foliage of towering bald cypress, magnolias, overhanging oaks, and sabal palms. People angling for bream or bass or catfish, seem, like us, to be more interested in their enchanting surroundings than fishing. This river is a must!

GENERAL RATING: XXXX
DIFFICULTY: MODERATE
SCENERY: EXCELLENT

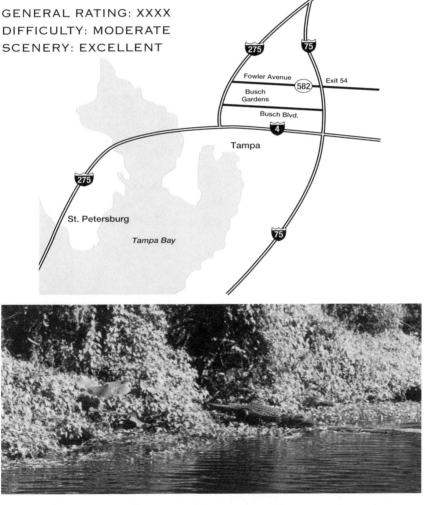

Hillsborough River

HOMOSASSA RIVER

The river, located in Citrus County, is a prime tourist attraction. Its source is a 55-foot-deep rocky spring that pours out 8,000,000 gallons of fresh water daily, and flows serenely for eight miles through the swamplands of Homosassa's rain forest and on out to the Gulf. People discovered the Springs in the horse-and-buggy days, and later traveled by rail to test its therapeutic powers. Homosassa, named by the original inhabitants, the Seminole and Calusa Indians, means "place of peppers," herbs gathered by the tribes for medicinal purposes. Tales of pirates, Indian massacres, moonshine, and bootlegging abound, including the saga of the MacRae family who came to Homosassa from Scotland and were among the area's earliest pioneers. They managed the Homosassa Inn, restored and operating today, and later thrived on the fishing industry. Their ancestors were among those who saw the railroad built to handle timber and fish shipments to various destinations. Today, "Gator" MacRae, as he's called, operates Duncan MacRae's bait house, which has been a fixture on the banks of the river since the turn of the century.

CANOE RENTALS

MACRAE'S
5300 Cherokee Way
Homosassa, FL 34467
(904) 628-2602

At this point, the MacRae family owns the only canoe rental on the river. It is situated on the Gulf Coast 80 miles west of Orlando, 60 miles north of Tampa. Take Exit 61 off I-75, and turn west toward Weeki Wachee. Go 22 miles on Highway 50 to Highway 19, turn north on 19 to Homosassa Springs, about 20 miles. In Homosassa Springs, turn left at the Burger King and follow the signs to the river. Once you're checked in, you're provided with a map of the area, but then you're pretty much on your own as, unassisted, you step gingerly into the old aluminum canoe which has been out-fitted and tied to the dock. Some may need help lowering themselves into the craft. It's a bargain, though, at only $7 for a half-day excursion, $12 for all day, or you can rent one by the hour at $2 per hour. The livery is open seven days a week, 7 a.m. to 6 p.m., and overnight accommodations are available at their motel. It's a quaint little fishing village, and locals like Gator love the area. "It's worth a lifetime living here," he says, "and if you get the chance, you'd enjoy living your life here all over again." The neighboring CANOE SAFARI does not solicit canoe rentals, offering only one canoe and a fleet of fishing and excursion boats.

CONCESSIONS

MacRae's office is small and rustic, and constantly busy because fishing is excellent, with redfish and trout abounding, and tarpon in season. The water is brackish where the Springs meet the Gulf waters. MacRae's supplies live bait, tackle, ice, and snacks. The restrooms are out in back, but they're clean and have sinks and running water. Restaurants and pubs line the river, so there's no shortage of convenient rest stops. It's worth your while, after your canoe trip, to stop at the site of the nearby ruins of an early sugar mill. For economic reasons, each plantation owned its own mill with wells that supplied water. The giant kettles, the cooling vats, deep storage pits, and the enormous boiler set into a stone furnace run by an iron steam engine were all operated by slave labor. These same slaves were responsible for cutting the cane before they processed it. The mill was owned by David Levy Yulee, the state's first U.S. senator. Yankees burned his home, but preserved the mill and the plantation.

THE TRAIL

If you want to get away from it all, this river is not the answer. You might call it a waterside bar-hopping expedition, because it's lined with picturesque inns, restaurants, and pubs whose wooden decks overlook the water.

After passing a tiny island, home to a tribe of vari-colored, volatile, and animated monkeys, we find that because of the commercial aspect of this section of the Homosassa with its heavy boat traffic, it's safer and more interesting to paddle close to the right shore which is mostly uninhabited. Great blue herons, roused from their nesting places in the heavy underbrush, rise and spread their giant wings, squawking in protest. Flocks of pelicans, snowy egrets, and anhingas perch everywhere. Shortly after we set out, we turn into an inviting, half-hidden little bayou where we find the stillness and wilderness we crave. It's a leisurely paddle, culminating in a cluster of rustic river homes. Once back on the wide river, after about a mile of paddling, we decide to follow the signs down another picturesque waterway to the Manatee Pub. There, the friendly owners serve us beers and invite us to enjoy our picnic lunch on their wooden deck overlooking the water where we can watch fishermen cleaning their catch. We don't sight one today, but the area is a haven for manatees, and the residents are militant about their no-wake signs. No one on the river is speeding. In all, our round-trip takes us about three hours of steady paddling, with time out for luxuriating in the splendor of the river and its many marinas and quaint fish houses.

GENERAL RATING: XX
DIFFICULTY: VERY EASY
SCENERY: FAIR

Homosassa River

OCKLAWAHA RIVER

We were confused about the two different spellings of this river, and were informed by Larry Reiche, owner and operator of the Canoe Outpost, that "Ockli-waha," which means "great and winding river," was the original spelling. Some 100 years ago, for unknown reasons, the "c" was omitted, but recently, local authorities petitioned the Post Office to return the "c". Some of the road signs and literature haven't yet gotten up to date. The Ocklawaha, said to be an ancient river, geologically, has deepened and widened considerably from its first trickle. It's one of the eight major rivers in the world that runs north. Before there were roads in the wilderness, it was used by shallow-draft, high-sided steamboats to transport supplies to settlers, and, later, passengers from St. Johns River to Silver Springs. We were told the area was once the site of several Civil War skirmishes. In the early 1900s, a ferry transported passengers from one side to the other. Because of its navigability, the river was pinpointed by the Florida Cross Canal project for use as a primary waterway. This decision resulted in prolonged controversy between environmentalists and the government, but, thankfully, many sections of this scenic river have been preserved. "The Oklawaha (sic) is the sweetest water lane in the world, a lane which runs for more than 150 miles of pure delight," wrote poet Sidney Lanier. (It is actually recorded to be 110 miles long.) It begins its flow in a series of lakes, which includes Lake Dora, Lake Griffin, and Lake Eustis, and winds through the western and northern boundaries of the great Ocala Forest, known as "The Big Scrub" by old-time crackers. The Ocklawaha flows for more than 60 miles in a northerly direction to St. Johns River, which forms the forest's eastern boundary. Its primary tributary is the Silver River, flowing from the popular tourist attraction Silver Springs.

CANOE RENTALS

THE OKLAWAHA OUTPOST
(the spelling will soon be changed)
Route 1, Box 1462
Fort McCoy, FL 32637
(904) 236-4606
Larry and Sylvia Reiche, owners/operators

Located in Marion County, 120 miles north of Tampa, 40 miles south of Gainesville, 100 miles north of Orlando, 300 miles north of Miami. From I-75, take Exit 70, go east on Highway 40 to SR 315 and travel north to Fort McCoy. Turn east on SR 316 and continue to the tall bridge that spans the Ocklawaha.

The sign advertising the Outpost can be seen on the north side of the road just before the bridge. The Outpost is open seven days a week, year-round, except for Christmas and Thanksgiving, 7:30 a.m. to 5 p.m. Reservations are required with a 50% deposit for all trips, and departure times are scheduled according to demand. The Outpost offers three trips: Gore's Landing to the Outpost: a distance of 8 miles, which takes 2–4 hours, $9.50 for adults, $4.60 for children under 12, a dollar charge for those under 6; Outpost to Cypress Bayou: 6.5 miles, 2–2.5 hrs., same fees; Silver River to Outpost: 18 miles, 5–6 hours, $11, $5.50, $1. Kayaks are also available.

CONCESSIONS

The Oklawaha Outpost is the only access to this scenic part of the river, and its decor is in keeping with the rustic flavor of the surroundings. It's small and primitive, but well-stocked with sandwiches, snacks, ice, camping supplies, bait and tackle, and other outdoor accessories. T-shirts are for sale along with hats, and Larry even has a sort of mini-museum displaying arrowheads, weapons, and other artifacts gleaned from the area. Restrooms are provided; hot showers and changing rooms can be used for a small fee. There's a free but cold outdoor shower for the more rugged canoeists. The Outpost also offers downstream raft and minnow trips. RV sites are available, and there is economy lodging nearby, specifically, the Springside Motel, clean, comfortable, and convenient. Camping gear can be rented if you want to rough it overnight for the specified two- or three-day trips. The nearby Silver Springs attraction is worth a visit to enjoy the crystal clear waters from glass-bottomed boats. All this, plus the picnic tables and other facilities, and the wondrous hiking trails of the Ocala National Forest!

THE TRAIL

We canoe this river the day after our Juniper Springs excursion, but the Ocklawaha trip differs in many ways. Here is the perfect water journey for pampered paddlers like ourselves. Our gear is loaded into a battered van by Larry, tall, lanky, bald, and muscular, and sporting a fierce-looking waxed mustache. He's Florida-born, a Navy veteran, friendly and accommodating, and loves the Ocklawaha. We're transported about eight miles through scenic back woods to Gore's Landing, where Larry hoists our canoe onto his broad back and sprints easily down to the launch site. He helps us into the canoe, and sends us off with a smile. "Just go with the flow," he reminds us, waving us off. (It's a good rule of thumb for almost all river trips.) As we glide along with the three- to five-knot current, we're immediately struck with the beauty of this canopied river. Here's one trip you can take even in hot weather because it's shaded for the most part by tall stately cypress, swamp maples, and sable palms, and Larry assures us there are not the usual number of stinging insects here. Several rope swings along the way have been fashioned for those who enjoy jumping into the water. These specified stops are well-marked, all the water is tannic-stained but pure, and the swimming areas are about as safe as you can get in the Florida waters although we're past the age of testing them. These canoes seem steadier and easier to manage than those we rented at Juniper Springs. Because there are fewer tortuous turns, we can lean against the back rests, sometimes just letting the current take us, to enjoy the sights. A sign reading "Dead River" invites us to explore a little arm of the Ocklawaha where the water is motionless, and only the calling of birds breaks the silence. We reach Cedar Creek, then return to the river. Except for an occasional powerboat carrying fisherfolk, and one intrusive airboat, we see little sign of humans. A giant turtle and a nearby alligator, sunning themselves on fallen trees, seem oblivious as we glide past. I am suddenly riveted by the sight of a huge snake coiling its considerable length and girth around the branch of a tree. (Afterward, Larry tells me I am one of the few who has spotted the elusive reptile, believed to be an escaped boa!) Happy to be safely out of reach in our canoe, we continue on, peering into the underbrush.

Gators, fully grown mammoths and their smaller offspring, their gray scales blending into their surroundings, sprawl across logs, legs dangling, to absorb the morning sun. A large colony of white ibis erupts from the bushes with a noisy flapping of wings, protesting our passage with great trumpeting. This is a wildlife bonanza! We see frisky otters, wild turkey, and all varieties of Florida birds. Even though we're not that fortunate today, some keen-eyed naturalists have reported seeing the Florida panther, bobcats, deer, and even black bears alone the shore. The river is home to more than 100 species of fish, 200 varieties of birds, and 300 different mammals. At a small sandy beach below a high bluff, we disembark to stretch our legs and eat our lunch. Underway once more, we savor the remaining miles of our excursion . . . the old Florida outback at its most beautiful . . . finally gliding under the towering bridge that spans the river to the Canoe Outpost sign that guides us to our destination. We pull our canoe up on the banks, abandon it and the gear, and, tired but fulfilled, trudge back through the woods to our car. It doesn't get any better than this. Don't miss it!

GENERAL RATING: XXXX
DIFFICULTY: EASY
SCENERY: EXCELLENT
A PAMPERED PADDLER'S PLUS !

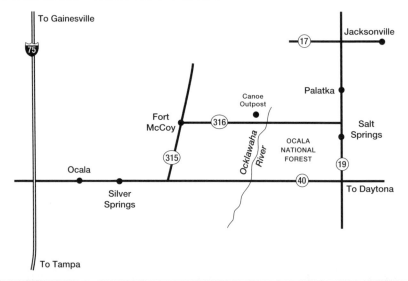

Ocklawaha River

PITHLACHASCOTEE RIVER

This rarely documented river, the River of the "Twin Richeys," is located in Pasco County. It bears a Creek Indian name meaning "canoes hacked out." Centuries ago, Seminole canoe builders traveled long distances to this particular body of water to carve their crafts from the giant, storm-toppled cypress trees. Narrow and winding, shallow and almost impassable in some areas, the trail was used almost exclusively for regional traffic.

CANOE RENTALS

D and R COTEE RIVER BAIT, TACKLE AND CANOE RENTAL
6241 Lincoln Street
New Port Richey, FL 34652
(813) 845-8330

You reach the launching spot by turning east on Main Street. Off US 19, drive over the bridge that spans the river, then turn right on Lincoln. The Pithlachascotee River is one of the reasons for our writing this book. We traveled 90 miles from Sarasota one beautiful, spring morning to navigate it, only to find there were no liveries in the area. It was then that we envisioned a handy guide to pinpoint waterways that offered canoe rentals. This newly opened facility offers an opportunity for recreational canoeists to explore one of Florida's best-kept secrets. D and R's is a small, unpretentious but clean operation, and offers bargain excursions. You can rent a fiberglass canoe for a half-day for only $8, $12 for all-day; $45 will get you a John Boat for all-day fishing, $30 for a half-day. You're assured by Jim Bolyard "the part-time flunky," as he calls himself, that "anything that swims in salt water, you can catch here." They're open from 6 to 6, seven days a week. It's easy launching, but the banks are muddy, not sandy, so wear old sneakers. With a few brief instructions, you're handed a whistle in case of emergency, life jackets, a tide table, and you're on your way.

CONCESSIONS

This is it! You can get snacks here, tackle, and live bait, and it's wise to avail yourself of the restroom because, as we discovered, there's no convenient place to stop unless you're desperate enough to slosh through mud. For this reason, go easy on liquids en route.

THE TRAIL

This is an urban trail that winds through part of the city of New Port Richey, but don't let that turn you off. Persevere, because once you get past the many charming and diversified homes that line the river, about 40 minutes of steady but leisurely paddling (the usual current measures only 0–1 mph), you suddenly leave civilization far behind with only the swish of your oars and occasional bird calls to break the intense silence. The winding river, at this point, seems deserted, and we don't encounter a soul for miles. The muddy banks give way to saw grass, palms, native oaks, cedars, and some gnarled giant skeletons of cypress trees. Downed monster timbers, victims of flooding, lie sprawled along the way, sometimes extending into our canoe's path. This calls for some tricky maneuvering, especially when the trail begins to narrow even more as we continue. The "Cotee," a shortened version of the Indian name used by locals, has tight curves, overhanging branches, and tangled shrubs in the upper segment, which demand some basic but challenging paddling. It widens to longer, straighter sections on the lower portion leading to the Gulf of Mexico, where you might encounter wind and waves if you have the stamina and the time to canoe that far. Turtles sun themselves on logs, and an inquisitive raccoon drinks at the water's edge. The river is a haven for manatees, anhingas, cormorants, all varieties of herons and egrets, scrub jays, and other smaller birds. The muddy flats spawn clams, scallops, and oysters, which can be harvested during designated seasons only.

We have our picnic in the canoe, floating with the gentle current, because of the uninviting mud on the shore. Be sure to bring a watch because you need to pace yourself on this trip according to your endurance. At some point it's necessary to turn around and paddle back, and there's that 40-minute trip past the river homes to consider. We choose to head back after two hours of steady paddling, a four-hour excursion in all. Everything looks different on the return trip, and to culminate our visual delight, we are privileged to spot the resident pair of bald eagles soaring overhead and circling for a few minutes before they fly away.

GENERAL RATING: XX
DIFFICULTY: MODERATE
SCENERY: EXCELLENT

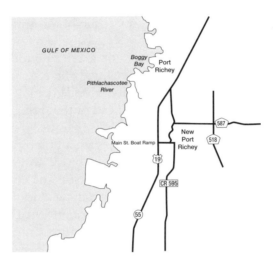

Pithlachascotee River

RAINBOW RIVER

It is located in Marion County in the Marion County K.P. Hole Park in Dunnellon. Once dubbed "Blue Run" or "Blue River" by locals because of its luminous blue shade, the name of this spring-fed waterway was changed to Rainbow River after it became a tourist attraction sometime in the late 1940s. Except for a brief period in the early 1700s, Native American Seminoles roamed the area into the mid-1800s when the first pioneers arrived and Florida became a state. They built a little town called Juliette at the head of the springs, and thrived for a time on their citrus groves. In 1890, because the fame of the temperate and therapeutic springs had spread, a hotel was built above the springs basin. By 1895, a succession of severe winters devastated the groves, but the purest phosphate deposits in the world were discovered soon afterward, and a prosperous mining era followed, which is still celebrated in Dunnellon with "The Boomtown Days Festival." All the while, behind the scenes, bootleggers were carrying on a brisk trade, brewing whiskey in the jungly growth along the river banks, and stories abound of treasury agents trying in vain to track them down in the wilderness. By the 1930s, with the addition of azalea gardens and manmade waterfalls, the head springs had become a destination resort. During World War II, the hotel facilities were used as an officers' club for glider pilots stationed at the Dunnellon Airport. The 55-acre site at the springs reached its heyday during the 1960s when the Holiday Inn and S&H Green Stamps took over joint ownership. Some of the existing structures are remnants of the attraction that closed in 1974. Today, more than 600 acres are preserved for the public's pleasure. All plant and animal life is strictly protected, and the rangers are militant in guarding the park grounds. As a result, the crystal clear Rainbow River is completely free of trash.

CANOE RENTALS

MARION COUNTY K.P. STATE PARK
9435 SW 190th Avenue
Dunnellon, FL 34432
(904) 489-3055
Sandra Fournier, Lead Cashier

Located 3 miles north of Dunnellon in Marion County, on the east side of US Highway 41, the facility is also accessible from points south on I-75: Take Exit 67, then turn left on Highway 485 West, 23 miles to the center of the town of Dunnellon, turn on to Highway 41 north at traffic light, and follow it out of Dunnellon (approximately two-and-a-half miles) to the Suwanee Swifty Store on the right. Take the second right after the store and follow it to the railroad tracks. Bear left one-half mile to the park entrance. It is also accessible from Highway 19. If you don't mind the rigid regulations governing this park, it's a pleasant and worthwhile trip for the entire family. Those in charge take the rules seriously concerning the ban of alcohol and pets. Although you're expected to haul your own canoe off the rack, Tom, a husky attendant, assures us he's on hand to help those who are not physically able to handle the crafts themselves. Equipped with the obligatory whistle issued for emergencies (the more laid-back liveries don't bother with them), we had little trouble toting our paddles and life vests, and launching our fiberglass canoe (the aluminum canoes are lighter and easier to handle) from the shallow water at the sandy shore, and were quickly on our way. You are responsible for sliding the canoe back onto its rack (if you are able) and for returning all rental equipment to the office. The livery is open daily, and a 2-hour canoe rental costs $7; 4 hours, $12; 8 hours, $20. A driver's license must be left as deposit. There is a charge for late returns. There are also giant inner tubes for rent for $3.50, but a leisurely float trip (approximately 3–4 hours) requires two vehicles of your own—one at the park, and one at the exit point next to Highway 484 in Dunnellon. We are reminded that Marion County is currently working on a shuttle service for canoeists and tubers alike. For those who wish to swim, there's a roped-off area at the canoe embarkation point and one at the springs, and if you like snorkeling or scuba diving, this is the place to bring your gear. The park is open from 8 to 8 summers, but during the winter season, canoes must be returned by 4 p.m. Tom is adamant about that, and also about the hours, carefully checking his watch as you set out. He also confides there are two closely guarded glass-bottom canoes under lock and key. As to who gets them, "it's a judgment call," he laughs. We were unable to wheedle him into giving us one.

CONCESSIONS

The K.P. (Knights of Pythias) Hole Park offers clean restrooms, showers, and changing rooms, and a tidy little concession stand sells snacks and cold drinks. Before we took off, we ate our picnic lunch on the wooden deck overlooking the water. After your excursion, the nearby Rainbow Springs Park, open daily from 8 a.m. until sunset, provides some pleasant moments. For $1 you can stroll the wide, brick paths, admire the 95-foot manmade falls cascading over rock formations, and take a bird's eye view of the beautiful Rainbow River. The Rainbow Springs campground itself has racks of canoes, but only for the convenience of its campers.

THE TRAIL

It's a pleasant change from gliding over the murky, tannin-stained waters of our previous trips to navigate the Rainbow River, fed by countless freshwater springs. Rather than constantly peering at the scenic shoreline or into the towering, moss-draped oak trees, we spend most of our time gazing down at the iridescent limestone and shell-littered sandy bottom. Sunlight transforms the depths to an

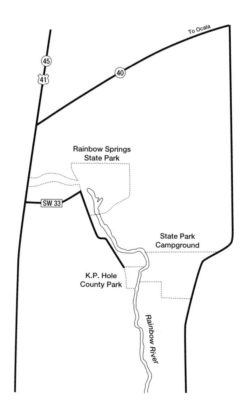

opalescent blue, and outlines masses of deep green eel grass tendrils flattened by the current. We're paddling upstream, it's true, but it's not much of an effort. Huge squawking herons, aroused by our passage, flap overhead, and cormorants and anhingas swim lazily across our bow. They know they're safe here in this refuge. Egrets cock their heads at us as they fish in the shallows or watch us from the branches of the trees. An 8-foot alligator, half-submerged in a patch of seaweed at the edge of the water, remains indifferent as we pass, while several baby alligators splash noisily nearby. Turtles, as always, are abundant, and we spot a pair of ospreys taking flight. The river floodplains and sandhill pine forest are home to many species of plants and animals. There are the usual riverside homes, but they don't intrude, and the silence, the beauty, the sense of traveling the wilderness, is unaffected by the evidence of civilization. It takes about forty minutes to reach the cul-de-sac that harbors the head springs. No fishing is allowed at this point. We delayed our return trip by just floating and gazing into the depths of the crystal-clear, year-round 72-degree waters. If you dive or snorkel, you need the red flag atop a pole to signal your presence. Going back with the current was a piece of cake in spite of the balmy headwind. This is an easy, scenic excursion, and requires few if any paddling skills.

GENERAL RATING: XX
DIFFICULTY: VERY EASY
SCENERY: GOOD

Rainbow River

SANTA FE RIVER

A tributary of the Suwanee River, its name means "Holy Father," so designated by early Spanish explorers. The Potano Indian tribe inhabited the lush area from approximately 10,000 B.C. until the Spaniards took control sometime in the 1600s. During the Second Seminole Indian War, from 1835 to 1842, the United States built four forts close to the river. The lower portion was used for commercial navigation in the early 1800s, and later on, a series of canals was dredged by the Santa Fe Canal Company. The unpredictable Santa Fe, curving for some 75 miles from Lake Santa Fe in Bradford County north of Gainesville until it meets the Suwannee, is almost impassable for the first 35 miles. It sinks out of sight at intervals, swallowed up by marshlands called the Santa Fe swamp, then pops back up in the form of a narrow, debris-filled rivulet. It becomes a pleasant, easily navigable stream in the O'Leno State Park, a region that covers Union, Columbia, and Alachua counties. At O'Leno, the cantankerous river disappears once more, flowing through subterranean passageways for several miles, and finally emerges above ground at the River Rise State Preserve as a clean, dark river lined with heavy foliage and punctuated by twelve crystal-clear springs scattered along the banks.

CANOE RENTALS

SANTA FE CANOE OUTPOST
Highway 441 at Santa Fe River Bridge (P.O. Box 592)
High Springs, FL 32643
(904) 454-2050

Because Jim and Sally Wood, the most recent owners of the SANTA FE CANOE OUTPOST located in Alachua County, offered to take us on both their Santa Fe and Ichetucknee River runs, we decided to spend several days in the area. Jim, big and husky and personable, and Johnnie, his affable and knowledgeable young assistant, manage the Santa Fe excursions that begin right at the Outpost. If you're traveling on I-75, take Exit 79 and turn west on 441 to High Springs. From High Springs, go west about two miles past the stoplight where 41 crosses 441. The Santa Fe Canoe Outpost's sign is located on the left side of the road just before the bridge that spans the river. The facility, which is open seven days a week, 8 a.m. until dark weekends, 9 a.m. until dark weekdays, offers all-day and overnight trips featuring top quality canoes, kayaks and gear. Reservations and deposits are required. Jim lists eight varied Package Programs, some of which include outdoor activities, overnight stays in rustic, dormitory-type lodgings, and meals. Each is priced accordingly. A romantic, guided Full Moon Tour is scheduled once a month at $14 a head. Arrangements can be made for corporate and organizational outings. We chose Trip 4, a popular seven-mile trip involving about three hours paddling time, which took us downstream to Rum Island past several of the many bubbling springs that originate in the vicinity. The cost is $22 for two occupants. Pampered Paddlers will appreciate the sturdy, steadier Osagian aluminum canoes, and that they're carried on Jim's sturdy shoulders down the wooden walkway to the water's edge. You follow, burdened only with the paddles and cushions and your own gear. You can travel downstream as far as you like, and pickup times are prearranged accordingly. If you take along one of Jim's trash bags and fill it at least half full of trash, he'll give you the next trip at half price. Whatever the reason, the rivers in this section of Florida are almost litter-free. We suggest weekdays for these trips because it's a popular resort area and gets crowded on weekends. In case you're interested, you can canoe as far as the Gulf of Mexico, about 90 miles, and use the primitive campsites along the way . . . in case you're interested.

OTHER CANOE RENTALS

ED'S CANOE OUTPOST
High Springs, FL

A small rental. No literature available, and it's not widely advertised, but we saw its location just off Main Street.

GINNIE SPRINGS
7300 NE Ginnie Springs Road
High Springs, FL 32643
(904) 454-2202, (800) 874-8571

STEAMBOAT CANOE OUTFITTERS, INC.
P.O. Box 28
Branford, FL 32008
(904) 935-1512

CONCESSIONS

Jim's Santa Fe Outpost is as rustic as you'd expect in this rural section of Central Florida, and his tin-roofed Snack Shack isn't always open. His outpost store does provide T-shirts, ice, sodas, snacks, and outdoor items, but it's best to bring your own lunch. The restroom is primitive and located outside the office, but it has running water and a sink. The accommodations at the lodge, which must be reserved in advance, consist of two bedrooms, a fireplace, a kitchen, and heat and air. Limited camping facilities located nearby cost $4 a head. The town of High Springs, once a bustling village that flourished during the 19th century along with the mighty railroad and its offshoot industry, went to seed when I-75 rerouted the traffic that had once flowed through it. It underwent a revival and a transformation to its turn-of-the-century look, thanks to intensive promotion by local entrepreneurs, and is now a delightful destination resort. A wealth of quaint antique stores and B-and-B inns, an Opera House, an excellent restaurant, called the Great Outdoors Trading Company, cater to the several thousand people who visit the nearby springs, rivers, and parks.

Nearby O'Leno State Park, Ginnie Springs, and the Ichetucknee State Park are favorite spots for hiking, tubing, and diving. Ginnie Springs Resort, about seven miles southwest of High Springs, has a $6 admission fee which includes swimming in its beautiful blue 72-degree waters. There are extra charges for canoeing, tubing, snorkeling, or diving to explore the many caverns (certified divers only) and awesome springs like Devil's Eye and Ear. Diving instruction is available, and there's a large general store displaying souvenirs, refreshments, and gear. Picnic tables, restrooms and shelters are scattered throughout the park, but it's worth the visit just to sit on the wooden deck on the edge of the springs and gaze down at the clear blue water. You can spot the divers spread-eagled on the bottom, their colorful wetsuits forming a vibrant kaleidoscope. If you can spend a few days in High Springs, you can hike the maze of bridges and trails where the Santa Fe goes underground at O'Leno State Park, or climb your way down the hundreds of stairs into one of Florida's deepest sinkholes at the Devil's Millhopper. It's a fascinating area.

THE TRAIL

NOTE: Although we prefer canoeing from November through April, this is a trail you can enjoy during the hotter months because there are so many inviting places to swim. If you're the hardy type, you can bring your suit even during the winter months. There are changing rooms in the parks. We love this excursion! The Santa Fe is wide and scenic and easy to paddle. Colonies of glistening slate gray turtles, perched on every available log or deadfall, scatter with a symphony of splashes as we pass. It's a balmy March day, and everywhere the forest is coming back to life, the ghostly winter-starved trees sprouting the first pale green buds of spring. The delicate hazy wash of color reminds us of an impressionist painting. We skim over sea grasses flattened by the current, past a sign that informs us we are entering the River Rise State Preserve. The water is the familiar deep coffee color, almost black-looking in the deeper sections of the river. The banks are crowded with pines, palms, and oaks, along with the tumbled, flood-ravaged remains of thousands of years of river growth. Sun-bleached cypress trees, tall and straight and stalwart as bearded, aging warriors, keep vigil on the banks.

We're alone with only the sounds of bird calls and the rippling of the water beneath our canoe. This is one of those dreamy, euphoric canoe trips that allows us to glide along now and then with the current . . . about two to three knots at most. Gators sunning themselves along the banks are scarcely visible, their gray scaly hides blending with tree trunks and mud. The roar of traffic at US 27 is only momentarily intrusive, and we paddle vigorously under the bridge, past the remains of an old railroad trestle, to lose ourselves once again in the wilderness.

At the five-mile point, we pull up to Poe Springs, a little park with a $3 entrance fee that entitles us to use the clear waters of the swimming area, the restrooms and picnic tables, and nature trails. Here we have a snack and take a brief, invigorating hike along the wooden walkway that leads through the swamp. Lily Springs isn't as well-marked, but we manage to spot the half-hidden entry and enter. Whimsical signs, erected by someone who calls himself, simply, "Ed," trace our passage. "This is a natural spring," we are reminded. "Please respect the nature you find here. Thanks." There's a thatched hut and several weather-beaten lawn chairs at the spring head, but today there's no sign of life. We're told later on that the springs are said to be a haven for nudists. Local lore has it that Rum Island, our next stop, was once the site of a whiskey still and a base for bootlegging operations. When we disembark to stretch our legs, I find, to my astonishment and delight, masses of violets half-hidden by the leaves that cover the marshy ground. My favorite flower, and one not ordinarily found in Florida! I pick a small bouquet and place it in the cooler for safekeeping. Reluctantly, we arrive at our pickup spot, but after lunch, we decide to canoe upstream a few miles to savor anew the scenic beauty of the Santa Fe. The current is almost nonexistent here, and it's a pleasurable bonus. It's hard to believe the scenery can vary so constantly, but the river continues to surprise us at every turn with the leafy patterns of the trees, the gnarled tree trunks, and fallen logs as mammoth and misshapen as storybook monsters. A two-hour ride is all we can manage this time. We're all paddled out!

GENERAL RATING: XXXX
DIFFICULTY: EASY
SCENERY: OUTSTANDING
A PAMPERED PADDLER PLUS!

Santa Fe River

SPECIAL ACCOMMODATIONS IN THE NORTH CENTRAL REGION

With so much mileage incurred with exploring Florida's canoe getaways, we find it necessary to spend a night or two in areas that contain more than one of the waterways listed in this guide. For exploring the north-central part of Florida, we chose a charming bed and breakfast called The Great Outdoors Inn, in the town of High Springs. It is under new ownership now, and is called THE RUSTIC INN. The same great service prevails.

THE RUSTIC INN
65 North Main Street
P.O. Box 387
High Springs, FL 32643
(904) 454-1223

The accommodations at THE RUSTIC INN, a non-smoking resort, are modern and beautifully decorated, with comfortable beds, lace-trimmed linens, roomy baths, air conditioning and heat, and paddle fans. There are six rooms, each a mini-getaway with a stocked refrigerator, and each with a different wildlife motif. We picked the Cat Room where even the bedspreads and the shower curtain are patterned with jungle cats. You can choose the Zebra Room or the Panda Room, among others. The new owner-managers, Larry and Diana, are sociable and totally concerned with your comfort. You can soak in the tub after your day of canoeing, stroll the nature trails on the 40 acres, or just sit and rock and watch the sunset from the little porch outside your room. Awaken the next morning to a breakfast basket of fresh muffins, fruit, spiced tea, and coffee. Rates are: Friday, Saturday, and holidays, $85; Sunday through Thursday, $75; one or two extra people in the room, $20. A deposit of one night's lodging is required and can be confirmed with a credit card. There are other quaint B&Bs in town and in the area, but THE RUSTIC INN was the ideal headquarters for us.

ICHETUCKNEE RIVER

The river is located in Suwannee and Columbia counties, but unlike its companion blackwater river, the Santa Fe, the Ichetucknee (pronounced "itch-TUCK-nee") is crystal-clear and unstained by tannic elements. Flowing southwest for six miles, it winds alternately through hammock and swamp before actually joining the Santa Fe. Its name is an Indian word meaning "pond of the beaver." You can see the teethmarks of the busy little creatures on the bases of tree trunks, which they have stripped of their bark. Long ago, Native Americans hunted and fished on this historic river, a Spanish mission was once located on its banks, and, in the early 1800s, a grist mill operated here. The Ichetucknee Springs was a popular rest stop for pioneer travelers on Bellamy Road, who pulled up to quench their thirst at its refreshingly cool, pure waters. At the turn of the century, phosphate was extracted from small surface mines, which are now almost obliterated by heavy foliage. Because of the former phosphate mining and logging activity, hardwoods have replaced parts of the open, grassy upland pine forest that once extended to within a few feet of the river banks. The Florida Park Service is attempting to restore and preserve the native plant community. Sandhills, located on the dry upland portions above the river, are home to fox squirrels, wild turkeys, deer, bobcats, and other wild creatures. There are nine named springs on the river, and their average total flow is about 233 million gallon of water daily. The water temperature remains at 73 degrees Fahrenheit year-round. Boiling out of limestone sinks or trickling out from cypress roots, over 100 springs, mostly unnamed, join to form this vitreous body of water with its white sand bottom.

CANOE RENTALS

SANTA FE CANOE OUTPOST
Highway 441 at Santa Fe Bridge
P.O. Box 592
High Springs, FL 42643
(804) 454-2050

GINNIE SPRINGS
7300 NE Ginnie Springs Road
High Springs, FL 32643
(904) 454-2202

**RIVER RUN
CAMPGROUND, INC.**
Route 2, Box 811
Branford, FL 32008
(904) 935-1086

**SUWANNEE OUTDOOR
ADVENTURE CENTER**
Post Office Drawer 247
White Springs, FL 3209
(904) 397-2347

STEAMBOAT CANOE OUTFITTERS
P.O. Box 28
Branford, FL 32008
(904) 935-0512

Jim Wood's SANTA FE CANOE OUTPOST was once more our choice for navigating the Ichetucknee. The canoes are sturdy and clean and easy to navigate, and the service is excellent. Today, Johnnie, the assistant, loads the canoes and gear on the trailer behind the van and shuttles us to the embarkation point, a twenty-five to thirty-minute ride. We're launched at 9 a.m. and agree upon a pick-up time of 11:30, which will allow us ample time to explore.

Containers of any kind containing food or drink are prohibited on the Ichetucknee, so we had a quick snack before we started out. Like the Santa Fe, the Ichetucknee is immensely popular, and we're happy we picked a less crowded weekday to observe wildlife undisturbed. The limited number of canoes at the ICHETUCKNEE SPRINGS STATE PARK rent for $20 each plus tax, and are available at either of the park entrances. The park is open from 8 a.m. until sunset year-round. The $4.25 entrance fee includes access to the swimming area and bathhouses. Theirs is a two-hour one-way trip from the north entrance, off SR 238, to the south take-out.

GINNIE SPRINGS is most famous for its cavern diving, but it also carries a limited number of canoes which rent for $5 for 2 hours, $10 for five hours, $16 for a full day.

CONCESSIONS

See Santa Fe River.

THE TRAIL

We're happy to note that the Ichetucknee, like its companion river, the Santa Fe, is almost entirely free of trash. As Johnnie insists, it's one of the cleanest waterways in the state due to regularly scheduled cleanups. When Johnnie carries the 65-pound canoe to the edge of the river, helps us launch it, and we're underway, we gasp with pleasure.

There's only one word for this body of water . . . breathtaking! The translucent waters of the Ichetucknee are a habitat for all manner of fish, clearly visible far below the surface as the bottom of our canoe scrapes across lime-colored tendrils of sea grass flattened by the two- to three-knot current. The countless springs that feed the river bubble up all around us. We make as little noise as possible with our paddles, trying not to disturb the scores of gopher turtles sunning themselves on logs and fallen tree limbs, and we're gratified to spot occasional wood ducks and a school of otters. Other familiar wading birds like ibis, herons, and egrets show no fear as we pass. Cavelike depressions carved into the limestone outcroppings by centuries of erosion loom ahead.

A stiff breeze sets the tall trees to creaking while a lone woodpecker keeps time. Floating lily pad gardens are splashes of lime green at the shoreline, a colorful contrast to the stately gray cypress trees with their goblin-like offshoots. We can't get enough of peering down at the iridescent blue patches of sand and limestone on the river bottom, or looking up at the varieties of birds perched in the trees. We stop at a tube-launching dock to stretch our legs, and walk a short way into the forest while a lone bird pipes its sweet song of welcome. En route once more, we paddle across wider, windswept sections of the river, and, although most of it is canopied, offering relief from the relentless Florida sun, we apply more sunscreen. We explore the crystalline springs, peer closely at the fenced-off habitats of manatees and rare snails, hoping to catch a glimpse of them, but today there is no sign, only silence. Because we're on a tight schedule, we reluctantly pull up to shore to wait for Johnnie. The trip can be prolonged for another two hours if prearranged. There are more springs further on. Pampered Paddlers who think they've seen it all, we still find the Ichetucknee a rare new experience.

GENERAL RATING: XXXX
DIFFICULTY: EASY
SCENERY: SPECTACULAR
A PAMPERED PADDLER PLUS!

Ichetucknee River

SUWANNEE RIVER

Various spellings of this classic river, most notably "Swanee" as depicted in the songs of the old South, have made it one of the most memorable. "Suwannee" is actually an ancient Cherokee Indian word, said to mean "echo." The river drains out of the Okefenokee Swamp just above Fargo, Georgia, and twists and turns its way across the Florida peninsula for over two hundred miles through numerous counties before it meets the Gulf of Mexico. A capricious river, it undergoes drastic changes in water levels throughout the year. Some of the hardier canoeists prefer the high tidewaters of late winter and spring, even the flooding that sometimes occurs in February and March, and welcome the faster current and the more turbulent rapids. At lower levels, in summer and fall, however, the beauty of the surroundings is more evident, and limestone caverns, grottos, and springs are revealed at the water's edge. There are 22 major springs on the river. Plan to spend a night there, as we did.

CANOE RENTALS

JIM HOLLIS'
RIVER RENDEZVOUS
Route 2, Box 60
Mayo, FL 32066
1-800- 533-5276

SUWANNEE CANOE OUTPOST
Route 1, Box 98A
Live Oak, FL 32060
1-800-428-4147

K.O.A. CAMPGROUND
P.O. Box 460
Old Town, FL 32680
(904) 542-7636

MANATEE SPRINGS STATE PARK
Route 2, Box 617
Chiefland, FL 32626
(904) 493-9726 (-9740, or -1197)

OTTER SPRINGS
R.V. RESORT
Route 1, Box 1400
Trenton, FL 32693
(904) 463-2696

RIVER RUN
CAMPGROUND, INC.
Route 2, Box 811
Branford, FL 32008
(904) 935-1086

SUWANNEE OUTDOOR ADVENTURE CENTER
Post Office Drawer 247
White Springs, FL 3209
(No Phone.)

There are many different segments of the river accessible to recreational canoeists. Your choice of canoe liveries depends on which is most convenient, because all the trips are scenic and worthwhile and similar in nature. Many of the liveries include several varying trips. We chose JIM HOLLIS' RIVER RENDEZVOUS in Lafayette County because we had to travel a long way, and his facility offered rustic but charming overnight accommodations. It is also home to Convict Springs, a crystal-clear swimming hole with a year-round temperature of 72 degrees. Follow Highway 27, 12.5 miles west of Branford, or 4 miles east of Mayo. Take Convict Springs Road north and follow the yellow signs. The livery is about 45 minutes from Gainesville, and 2 hours from the Jacksonville Airport. If you're traveling on I-75, take Exit 78. Jim Hollis is affable, accommodating, and knowledgeable about the area springs and the excellent diving opportunities. Canoes rent for $3 an hour, and there is a $3 drop-off fee if you choose the 3-hour trip that meanders downstream back to the Rendezvous. You may choose the 5-hour trip and paddle down to Branford, which involves a $5 pick-up fee. $20 gets you an all-day rental. Be advised that life jackets and paddles are provided for the easily maneuverable aluminum canoes, but no cushions or backrests. Bring your own if you feel the need.

CONCESSIONS

Jim Hollis has it all: tent sites, boat charters, diving trips, sauna and steam rooms, and a giant portable hot tub. He and Cheryl Owen, a charming lady, keep the place open seven days a week year-round. You can swim in Convict Springs or enjoy a barbeque at the water's edge. There's even a rifle range, a restaurant serving home-cooked meals, a bar with a gameroom and lounge, and overnight accommodations ranging from a bunk house to an A-frame with a fireplace overlooking the river. Credit cards are accepted, and pay phones are available on the property. Lafayette County (locals insist on pronouncing it La-FAY-ette) is a dry county, and only beer and wine coolers are served, so if you feel the need of a stronger libation at the end of the day, bring your own.

THE TRAIL

At the embarkation point, this section of the Suwannee is wide and placid, with limestone outcroppings at the water's edge, and winterized bearded oaks leaning out from the five-foot-high bluffs. It's silent on this brisk, sunny January day, and the trees, stripped of their leaves, look ghostly and beautiful with their silvery feathery-looking clusters of branches. The brilliant green of the lily-pad gardens below the banks are spots of more vibrant color. Only the raucous complaint of crows accompanies us as we start out, but we soon spot colonies of turtles, herons, and a pair of eagles descending to perch on the top of a tree high above. Wildlife is not so evident this time of year, but we're told that in warmer weather it's abundant, and almost every native Florida tree can be found at some point on the Suwannee.

Because the river is still low, we paddle close to shore to admire the many caves and grottos, but we're on the lookout for sharp

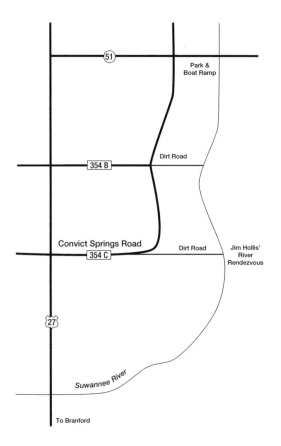

rocks that emerge from the water, and we steer judiciously clear, sometimes navigating carefully between large masses of them, enjoying the occasional eddies and "rapids" that form around them. There's a sprinkling of river camps, scarcely visible behind the trees on the bluffs. Only scattered bits of trash are regrettable reminders of man's disrespect for this God-given beauty. We stop to admire Bathtub Springs, a pool of crystal-clear water with a little waterfall pouring over the stones, and pass by the towering Drew Railroad Bridge. Although the bridge itself is gone, the iron mechanism, once turned by hand by two men, is rusted but intact. It was built by the Drew Sawmill Company in 1819 to transport lumber from the old logging road in Mayo to the logging town of Live Oak, and operated until sometime in 1902 to allow paddlewheelers, ferries, and other river boats to pass beneath it. We picnicked on one of the level limestone outcroppings on the banks, stretched our legs, then continued our leisurely and pleasant way back to the camp. A relaxing soak in the hot tub, a few low-level alcoholic drinks, a fine meal, and a good night's sleep conclude our delightful visit with this segment of the Suwannee.

GENERAL RATING: XXX
DIFFICULTY: EASY (DOES INVOLVE SOME TRICKY MANEUVERING AT LOW LEVELS TO AVOID ROOKS).
SCENERY: GOOD

Suwannee River

TOMOKA RIVER

The Tomoka River originates in a narrow coastal region between the Halifax River lagoon and the St. Johns valley in Volusia County, a few miles west of Ormond Beach and north of Daytona. The river loops northward for some thirteen miles through a historic section of the state. In 1605, a brochure states, the Spanish governor of Florida sent an expedition led by Alvaro Mexia to explore the east coast south of St. Augustine. The men followed trails to the village of Nocoroco, built by the Timucuan Indians at the site now occupied by the Tomoka State Park. The Spaniards named the stream "Rio de Timucuas" (River of the Timucuans). After Florida was acquired from Spain by the British in 1763, the publication goes on to say, the area became part of the vast land-grant holdings of Richard Oswald, a wealthy Scottish merchant and statesman who helped negotiate the treaty with England following the American Revolution. It was perhaps then that settlers found it simpler to pronounce "Timucuan" or "Tomoka." Indigo, the source of a popular blue dye during Colonial years, was planted in forest clearings, while rice and sugar cane were grown in the marshlands. The Timucuan Indians, who inhabited the area nearly 400 years ago, vanished with the onslaught of civilization.

CANOE RENTALS

TOMOKA STATE PARK
2099 North Beach Street
Ormond Beach, FL 32174
(904) 676-4050

Drive east on SR 40 through Ormond Beach, then turn north on Beach Street. Continue three miles north to the TOMOKA STATE PARK entrance where there's an entrance fee of $3.25 per vehicle. As of this writing, the park offers the only access to the river for those who don't own their own canoes, although some of the rangers expressed a desire to see a launch site for the general public farther up the river where paddling is easier and more scenic, and includes a wilderness stretch of the river that was the site of one of the old "Tarzan" movies. When we canoed the river in March of 1996, the park was in the process of improving the facilities, and by the time this book appears on the shelves, canoeists will be able to launch their craft directly at the water's edge. Park personnel assure us that those who need help with canoes can be assisted by one of the rangers, but as is the case in most state parks, you're mostly on your own. Park hours are 8 a.m. to sundown, but canoes should be returned by 5 p.m., so time your trip accordingly. At present, there are 10 long aluminum Grumann canoes for rent at $3 per hour or $15 per day, and no kayaks.

CONCESSIONS

The rental office is located in the gift store, which also sells snacks, cold drinks, and ice. The adjacent bathhouse has clean, modern restrooms, and there are five picnic areas. Swimming is not permitted in the rivers within the park, and alcoholic beverages are prohibited. The park also offers ranger-conducted tours, camping, nature trails, fishing, and boating. A collection of Fre Dana Marsh's artwork is housed in the museum bearing his name. There are many nearby state parks to visit. The Bulow Plantation Ruins State Historic Site in Bunnell, about six miles northeast on Old King's Road, once boasted the largest sugar mill in the state of Florida, and is well worth the $2 visit. In 1821, Major Charles Wilhelm Bulow acquired 4,675 acres of Florida wilderness that eventually bore his name. Using slave labor, he cleared his vast acreage and planted various crops. Even though Bulow befriended the resident Seminoles, the Indians, feeling threatened, became more hostile, and Bulow and other settlers abandoned their plantations and followed the troops northward. In 1836, the Seminoles burned "Bulowville" and surrounding plantations to the ground. All that remains are the massive, charred coquina ruins of the sugar mills, its wells, and the areas that housed the giant kettles.

THE TRAIL

Because the new launch site is not yet available, a friendly ranger manages to find us a canoe and starts us out. It's an easy paddle downstream on picturesque Strickland's Creek, which is a manmade canal dredged in the '50s to aid in mosquito control. Even so, the shoreline is wild and scenic. Once we reach the brackish Tomoka River, it's strenuous going upstream on the wide, windswept waters. It's perfect for testing your paddling skills, but make sure you're in good physical shape, wear a hat that won't blow off, and apply sunscreen because there's little shade . . . just a vast expanse of coastal marshland, with mangroves, cedars, palms, and oaks clumped beyond the sandy shoreline. Patient fisherfolk, their small powerboats anchored near the edge of the river, wait for unwary redfish or trout. Coffee-colored tidal creeks and shallow lagoons beckon along the way, and we venture in to explore, carefully skirting the mudflats. We find a sandy beach on which to stretch our legs and enjoy our lunch, noting the oyster shells that litter the sand, remnants of Indian middens that abound in the area. You can travel 10 or more miles along the Tomoka, which becomes narrower and even more scenic, twisting its way around cypress knees. We chose a five-hour roundtrip, pacing ourselves for the return trip.

GENERAL RATING: XX
DIFFICULTY: STRENUOUS UPSTREAM, MODERATE DOWN-
STREAM
SCENERY: GOOD

Suwannee River

WEKIVA RIVER

Located in Orange County, in the Orlando area, the river's source lies in the Wekiwa Springs State Park. (The waterway goes by two spellings, "Wekiwa" and "Wekiva." From I-4, take the Sanford Exit 51. The river flows north for fifteen miles to the St. Johns River. Today, the pristine, spring-fed Wekiva River at Orlando's back door appears much the same as it did 4,000 years ago when Native Americans such as the Creeks lived there. Discovered by Spanish explorers, the river was named by the Timucuan Indians, and literally means "a place to live on clear water." In 1875, vessels of the Wekiva Steamship Company navigated the waterway to transport the U.S. mail, citrus, building materials, and other cargo between what is now Wekiwa Springs State Park and Jacksonville. In the 1880s, a tourist hotel, proclaiming the healing waters of the Springs, then known as "Ford Springs," was opened, and bottled water was sold commercially as a cure-all. With the addition of a dance pavilion, water slides, and excursion boats, it very likely became the first "amusement park" in Central Florida. During that era, the Sanford to Leesburg wagon trail and "ford" was replaced by a railroad with a timber trestle that spanned the Wekiva. Northern passengers arriving on large sidewheelers would transfer to the train for a scenic trip past the Gulf Coast of Tampa. A section of the trestle still stands, and can be seen on your canoe excursion. The river contains one of Florida's richest concentrations of Ice Age fossils, and recent discoveries included an eight-foot mammoth tusk. Ancient animal teeth and other treasures continue to emerge from digging in the waters and limestone caverns in the area.

CANOE RENTALS

WEKIVA FALLS MARINA, INC.
1000 Miami Springs Road
Longwood, FL 32779
(407) 862-9640

KATIE'S WEKIVA RIVER LANDINGS
190 Katie's Cove
Sanford, FL 32771
(407) 628-1482

We chose to embark from KATIE'S WEKIVA RIVER LANDINGS on the St. Johns River, which offers the most diverse trails. It's only

22 miles from downtown Orlando, and located 5 miles west of I-4 off SR 46. From Mount Dora, travel east on SR 46 for approximately 12 miles. The livery, operated by Katie for over 20 years, is located on the northeast side of the bridge, and provides shuttle service for any of the river runs. Katie's downstream excursions offer a wide choice, depending on your ability, interest, and stamina, and include:

THE LITTLE WEKIVA

Nine miles long and the most popular trail, the first 4 miles are on the pristine and primitive Little Wekiva, the last 5 on the Wekiva, which is wider and has more river traffic. Paddling time is anywhere from three-and-a-half hours to five, at a cost of $12. Departure times are 8 and 9:30 a.m., 11 a.m., noon, and 1 p.m.

ROCK SPRINGS RUN

An all-day adventure for the hardy for $15, not to be considered if you don't want to camp out.

ST. JOHNS RIVER RUN

This shorter route is 6 pleasant miles on a narrow waterway, scenic with overhanging trees, and takes only 2 to 3 hours. It involves only the lower basin of the river from the landing to Emanuel Landing. Pick-up times at your destination are 3 and 5 p.m.

BLUE SPRINGS RUN

From the landing to Blue Springs State Park on the St. Johns, it's the same 6-mile trip on the St. Johns as the preceding run with an additional 6 miles on the river ending up at the park (famous for its "wintering manatees"), a total of approximately 5 to 6 hours. Pick-up times at your destination are 4 and 6 p.m. We strongly recommend weekdays for this one as the boat traffic is heavy here on weekends. The owners request that you arrive 15 minutes before your scheduled departure time. Group rates are available, and children 3–12 years old can canoe half-price. NOTE: Firearms are not permitted on any of the canoe trips.

CONCESSIONS

It's worth spending an additional day here to enjoy the naturally heated 74-degree waters of the the nearby springs in the famous Wekiva Falls Campground, and its many other amenities. The State

Park offers hiking on the scenic trails and lookout points. Katie's Landing, a rustic, well-equipped livery, stocks the usual snacks, gear, souvenirs, and supplies, and its restrooms are well maintained. Katie's also has a five-acre campground accommodating RVs as well as tents, and rents out several log cabins at the river's edge. You can get a delicious lunch or dinner, and libations, Tuesday through Sunday at the COCK OF THE WALK restaurant overlooking the river at the nearby Wekiva Marina.

THE TRAIL

Katie's canoe runs are leisurely day trips on the Wekiva River and its tributaries. The upper portion of the Wekiva has been designated an aquatic preserve; the lower basin is described in brochures as "scenic and wild." "The area hasn't changed since Ponce De Leon and his soldiers explored it," Katie claims. The area is ideal for picnicking, swimming, fishing, photography or simple enjoyment. We chose the popular nine-mile Little Wekiva Run on a sunny day in

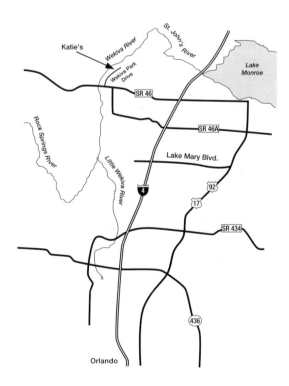

March, our favorite time of the year for canoeing. The coffee-colored waters of the Wekiva River twist through pine and hardwood uplands and dense swamplands, and pass through the lower Wekiva State Preserve before flowing into the St. Johns River. The old railroad trestle is a good spot to disembark for a picnic lunch. There are a table and benches on the high bank for our convenience where we can enjoy the beautiful view and watch an occasional canoe pass below. The Wekiva narrows and becomes deeper in some sections, and a current, though sluggish, is evident. Twisted branches and heavy foliage form canopies over much of this trail, adding to its utter quiet and privacy. Four miles of dense swamp accompany our trip through the Lower Wekiwa River State Park Preserve before the river widens once more and the St. Johns River comes into view. It's not recommended that inexperienced canoeists venture out on this body of water. It is said to involve strenuous paddling, often accompanied by high winds, choppy water, and heavy traffic, especially on weekends. We stick to the scenic section of the river, which is an unspoiled wilderness with endless varieties of wildlife.

GENERAL RATING: XXX
DIFFICULTY: EASY
SCENERY: GOOD

Tomoka River

WEEKI WACHEE RIVER

The name is a Creek Indian name meaning "little spring," but it is, in reality, a major spring which creates a swift current in its upper six miles. It is located in Hernando County, in the section of Florida known as the Nature Coast, west of Brooksville and south of Tampa. One hundred cubic feet of year-round 72-degree water of unusual clarity bubbles continuously from a large spring rising from the limestone bottom of the headwaters of the river, a novelty which created a famous underwater tourist attraction on the site. The wilderness section of the Weeki Wachee is a canoeist's and fisherman's paradise, but can only be reached by paddling upstream against the current. The river is a haven for manatees, and locals are fiercely protective of them. Its location on the Nature Coast recalls the Native Americans, Turbaned Indians, who fished and hunted the area long before the first Europeans discovered what they called the New World. As late as the mid-1800s, Seminoles continued their war against the coastal settlers before they were forced to leave the productive land.

CANOE RENTALS

WEEKI WACHEE MARINA
7154 Shoal Line Blvd.
Weeki-Wachee, FL 34607
(904) 596-2852

The marina is located west of Brooksville and north of Tampa. If you take I-75, use Exit 61 and travel west on 98 to Brooksville, then take SR 50 to US 19, cross over 19 and proceed to Highway 595 which is Shoal Line Boulevard. Turn left (south) two miles to the bridge that spans the river. Weeki Wachee Marina is located across the bridge just off the road on your left. It's open year-round except for bad weather, but it's always best to call and make reservations. To date, it's the only livery on the river, and rents about 25 Mohawk fiberglass canoes and a few kayaks. The canoes rent for $20 a day, $15 half-day, $12 for three hours, which includes cushions, paddles, and life jackets; kayaks rent for $25 a day, $18 half-day, $5 for three hours. A county ordinance forbids alcoholic beverages. The sturdy canoes are heavy, but are lowered into the water for you below the pier. You may need a little help clambering down into the craft, and someone to steady it while you take your elected position.

CONCESSIONS

The office is located in a small but well-stocked store offering the usual tackle, bait, ice, soft drinks, snacks, and souvenirs. The Marina also handles boat and motor sales. Restrooms are outside the store, but have running water, and are tidy. The nearby tourist mecca, world-famous Weeki Wachee Springs, open 365 days a year, offers many diversions including picnic grounds, swimming, tubing, and popular underwater shows viewed from glass-bottomed boats. Bring your bathing suit on this trip if you like, because the spring-fed, temperate waters are a favorite for diving, snorkeling, and swimming. There's also a roped-off swimming area in the little park near the marina. Across the river is Otters, a rustic restaurant overlooking the river, a pleasant place to dine.

THE TRAIL

This river is a busy one, especially on weekends, so definitely plan a weekday trip. It's a Sunday, and all manner of craft join us on course, but power boats obediently maintain a slow speed as the "No Wake" signs direct. We paddle past picturesque little river homes, and a family of colorful, vociferous wood ducks circling their watery domain. The swimming area to our left is crowded with bathers taking advantage of the balmy March day. This heavily populated leg of our journey is made pleasurable by the fact that there are no signs of civilization in the tropical jungle to our right, which is identified as Southwest Florida Water Management Territory. We see several groups of divers exploring the myriad springs that bubble up all around us. It should be noted that navigating the Weeki Wachee involves paddling upstream against a rather swift current. Unless you're prepared for strenuous exercise, don't try this one. For our part, we like the extra effort. When we arrive at the river, we bear right as we've been advised. The narrow waterway is heavily canopied, the trees newly green and offering plenty of shade, but we apply sunscreen just in case. It takes us about 45 minutes of steady, vigorous paddling to reach a stretch of wilderness where, at last, we can enjoy gazing down into the clear water with its white, sandy bottom and graceful river grass. We've been told we can paddle the entire eight miles of the Weeki Wachee up to the springs if we're able, but we're finally overcome by exhaust fumes from the many Sunday power boaters, and reluctantly turn back. In spite of its commercial character and shoreline housing, it's a beautiful river with water oaks, palm trees, and cypress, home to many varieties of wading birds and ospreys. On the return trip, we're propelled by the swift current and the light breeze at our backs, and shoot back in record time. We figure the current to be about five knots. We're rewarded near the end of our journey by the sight of a giant manatee, easily visible in the translucent depths, swimming underwater next to our canoe. Aside from that, we've seen little wildlife. Not exactly a back-to-nature trip experience, but pleasant nevertheless!

GENERAL RATING: XX
DIFFICULTY: MODERATE TO STRENUOUS
SCENERY: GOOD
NOTE: We repeat—Try this one on a weekend, be prepared to maneuver out of the way of boats both oncoming and overtaking, and get in shape for some vigorous paddling.

Weeki Wachee River

WITHLACOOCHEE RIVER SOUTH

Meandering through Citrus, Hernando, Marion, Pasco, and Sumter counties, this winding river, over 100 miles long, is supposedly named after its northern sister, a Georgia river originating northwest of Valdosta and flowing about 70 miles through the coastal plain to the Florida border. The two rivers are, in fact, separated by many miles, and are totally unalike. Most of the Withlacoochee River North is rugged, and not recommended for Pampered Paddlers. Seminole Indians once used the Withlacoochee River South for hunting and fishing. The waterway, which flows from south to north from its source, the Green Swamp near Lakeland, and on out to the Gulf, is said to mean, appropriately, "long and winding waterway." Although the nearby town of Nobleton was once railroad territory, bridges over the river are rare, and a lone trestle is all that marks the site of Fort Dade, a stronghold during the 19th century Indian wars when white men fought to drive the Seminoles away from their homes. Another landmark is what remains of an iron bridge used to haul cypress logs from St. Catherine to the main line in Croom.

CANOE RENTALS

NOBLETON BOAT RENTAL
P.O. Box 265
Nobleton, FL 34661
(904) 796-7176

BIG BASS RESORT
P.O. Box 28
Istachatta, FL 34636
(904) 796-3784

TURNER'S CAMP
3033 Hooty Point
Inverness, FL 32650
(904) 726-2685

ANGLER'S RESORT
12189 S. Williams Street
Dunnellon, FL 34421
(904) 489-2397

FLORIDA CAMPLAND, INC.
21710 Highway 98 North
Dade City, FL 33525
(904) 583-2091

THE CANOE OUTPOST
P.O. Box 188
Nobleton, FL 34461
(904) 796-4343

BAGGETT'S WITHLACOOCHEE
R.V. PARK AND CANOE RENTAL
P.O. Box 114
Lacoochee, FL 33537
(904) 583-4778

There are so many variations of this particular canoe trip, it would be difficult to cover them all, but the location we think is most pleasant to navigate is in Nobleton, Florida, in Hernando County, and we chose THE CANOE OUTPOST, whose owners sent us some interesting literature. Take I-75 to Exit 54, then turn east on Highway 582 until you reach Highway 301. Then turn north, and drive approximately nine miles to the park entrance. Or, if it's convenient, get on I-75, and take Exit 62 (Webster), go west approximately three-and-one-half miles to a stop sign. Turn left (west) and proceed four miles on Route 476 to the bridge spanning the river. Cross the bridge and travel about one-quarter mile. You'll see the blue sign with the canoe logo, and the CANOE OUTPOST sign.

The OUTPOST has been managed by Debby and George Blust for the past sixteen years, and because it has existed since 1976, it is a little bit of history in itself. The Grauman aluminum rental canoes have seen some knocking about in their day, but they're watertight and easy to maneuver. The livery is open from 8:30 a.m.–6 p.m. weekends, and until 5 p.m. weekdays except Tuesday. The Blusts advise you to call ahead for reservations and ask that you check in one-half hour before departure. Firearms and dogs are prohibited. (Dogs attract gators, they tell us.) We decided on the 5-mile excursion, which takes about two hours at a cost of $20 per canoe, and picked a starting time of 10:30 a.m. You can also take a 10-mile trip, 3–5 hours for $23; a 16-mile trip, 5–6 hours for $26. The canoes are equipped with paddles, life jackets, and cushions. Dry-boxes to store your equipment can be rented for $2, and backrests for $1. You can check out the canoes by the hour if you wish, for $4 an hour with a 2-hour minimum, or $17 for an all-day excursion on your own. We chose the package deal, paddling to Hog Island from the launching site, and on back to the Outpost. A unique little bonus is the "Float Diary," standard issue with every trip, guiding you into the wonderful world of the Withlacoochee. For the scheduled trips, you are transported to the launching sites by van, passing through the tiny town of Nobleton—population: all of 117! Many of the original houses built for the railroad workers remain. You pass the Croom Wildlife Management area and the Withlacoochee

State Forest before you're sent on your way with able assistance and brief instructions.

CONCESSIONS

The Blusts don't sell snacks, but the River Oaks Market and Country Store next door can provide you with food and refreshments. We suggest you bring your own cooler, binoculars, camera, and a compass because there's lots to see en route. The Outpost can completely outfit you if you are one of those who enjoy camping out, and it offers lengthier and more difficult trips for experienced and adventurous canoeists. The restroom, located in an outside shed, is rustic but clean and comfortable, with running water and a sink to freshen up. The only other modern facilities are at the Hog Island Campground more than an hour away.

THE TRAIL

It's a beautiful November day, sunny and just crisp enough for pleasant paddling. This waterway, we feel, is one of the top ten "easy Florida rivers." John, seated in his usual position in the stern, expertly steers the canoe as we glide along with the slow current. Now and then, we just float, lean back, and enjoy. Today, Withlacoochee waters are high and navigable and as smooth as glass. We're told that the water is generally only four to six feet deep, and even if, God forbid, you should capsize, there's little danger except for ruining your gear and your pride. After we paddle past a cluster of canoes bearing a troop of local Boy Scouts, there's little sign of life, only a few lone fishermen, and occasional silent, devout canoeists like ourselves. Cypress giants line the river, with their myriad knobby knees rising from the tannin-stained waters at their feet. Fall is evident here in Florida, the leaves of the lichen-covered oak and bald cypress trees turned to gold and rust by the recent cold weather. Their reflections in the glassy water are sheer beauty. We pass a young gator sunning itself on a partly submerged log with flocks of ibis, pecking for food, visible in the dense undergrowth behind it. Egrets suddenly explode into the air like a flurry of giant snowflakes. A lone hornet's nest dangles unchallenged from an overhead branch. All the while, we breathe in the rich, pervading odor of damp marshlands. Birds break the silence, signaling back and forth to each other, and we spy an osprey nest in the branches of a towering cypress. The osprey parents circle protectively as we pass, then disappear. As we paddle into Hog Creek, the halfway mark, and enter the crooked little byway, an eight-foot alligator, half-hidden in the pickerel weed and water hyacinths, opens one sleepy eye, perhaps lazily contemplating a late-day snack of mud turtles resting on a nearby fallen tree trunk. We eat our lunch at a picnic table, watching young boys fishing off the sandy banks. One proudly shows us his heavily laden stringer. The river abounds with freshwater fish including bream, bass, catfish, and pickerel. A fishing license is required if you're 15 or older. We pass the landmark remains of the railroad trestle, but it's only near the conclusion of the trip that we see river homes with their docks and boats, and are reminded that civilization is always nearby. Until then, it's been a silent communication with nature at its best.

GENERAL RATING: XXXX
DIFFICULTY: EASY
SCENERY: EXCELLENT

Withlacoochee River

JUNIPER SPRINGS

This excursion originates in the JUNIPER SPRINGS RECRE-ATIONAL AREA in the Ocala National Forest in Marion County. Constructed in the 1930s by the Civilian Conservation Corps (CCC), the maze of manmade waterways provides access to semi-tropical scenery unlike any found in other National Forests throughout the country. With additional water from Fern Hammock Springs, the daily flow is about 13 million gallons, with a 72-degree water temperature year-round. The Juniper Springs springhead is enclosed in concrete, providing a crystal-clear swimming pool below the concession stand. A waterwheel, once used to generate electricity, is powered by the force of the water flowing from the pool.

CANOE RENTALS

JUNIPER SPRINGS CANOE RENTALS
24860 NE 147th Place
Fort McCoy, FL 32134
(904) 625-2808

Juniper Springs is located 22 miles east of Silver Springs. Take Ocala/Silver Springs Exit 68 from I-75. From Ocala, travel east on SR 40 to the Juniper Springs Recreational Area. The entrance fee is $2.25, and signs direct you from the gate to the canoe rentals located on the water's edge. Hours are Monday to Friday, 9 a.m.–noon, Saturday and Sunday, 8 a.m.–noon. These times are written in stone, so come early to avoid getting bumped. Even reservations are honored until 10 a.m. "only," and deposits are non-refundable. A $20 refundable deposit is required at the time of rental along with the $21.25 fee for a 15-foot canoe, (2–3 persons), $24.25 for a 17-footer (7 persons). The price includes paddles, life jackets, and return transportation for people and canoes. (Credit cards not accepted.) You are responsible, they warn, for the equipment until it has been checked back in. There is an overtime charge of $5 per 15 minutes if you don't return by 5 p.m. The rigid regulations include no wading, floats, rafts, or inner tubes (to avoid snakes or possible alligator attacks, we're told), and no disposable containers. Be advised that this is another of those do-it-yourself trips involving some physical exertion. You are responsible for loading your own canoe onto a cart, pushing it down to the water's edge, then returning to the office where you pick up your paddles and the rest of your equipment. At the conclusion of the trip, you must return all gear to receive your refund. If you're not physically able to manage this, don't do Juniper Springs.

CONCESSIONS

Telephones, showers, and changing rooms are provided along with restrooms—not too tidy, but reasonably clean. The usual camping supplies, snacks, ice, souvenirs, and fishing tackle can be purchased at the concession stand. A 79-unit campground is open year-round, and offers hiking, picnicking, snorkeling, and bird-watching. A visitor center is located in the "Old Mill House" on the premises, which displays a waterwheel and depicts the area's development and wildlife. You can purchase homemade jams and jellies and other condiments there. This section of the Ocala National Forest contains a 66-mile section of the Florida National Scenic Trail.

THE TRAIL

A seasoned canoeist once told us that Juniper Springs was "the canoe trip from hell," but it's nothing compared to creeping through the mangrove tunnels of the Everglades, or struggling across vast expanses of windswept lakes. While it's definitely not a trip for senior citizens with heart trouble or other serious disabilities, it's a challenging and exciting experience. The most difficult segment is the initial, rather intimidating two-mile stretch. After we launch our own canoe (we're in good shape so the exertion doesn't faze us), we find the water is clear but shallow at first, narrow and rife with obstacles. If you're corpulent, cross this trip off your list because there's no way you'll be able to slide under the fallen trees that block your way even if you lie prone in the canoe the way we do. It's also important to know that these particular canoes don't seem as stable as most, and every sharp encounter with a protruding log or branch causes it to tilt dangerously. (En route we do indeed witness a canoe capsizing.) Because of this, we use extreme caution, and are prepared to do a few acrobatics as we navigate the difficult twists and turns and the swift current. In the bow, eagle-eyed, constantly alert for obstacles, I make the judgment calls, and John steers accordingly. When we finally get accustomed to the tricky maneuvers (not without a bit of bickering, we admit), we're able to take in the endlessly changing, magnificent vistas. The forest of cypress and palms and dense underbrush closing in on us from either side is a haven for wildlife that appears unafraid of humans. A raccoon poses patiently for our camera; turtles, large and small, looking sleepy and bored, remain on their beds of logs; a school of sleek otters frolics in the water near our craft. A green sign erected in the water alerts us to the fact that we've arrived at the halfway mark, a wooden dock about 200 yards ahead. We eat our lunch here under the watchful eye of an osprey perched high in the branches above. Once we're underway again, the stream widens and becomes easier to navigate. We round a bend and surprise a 16-foot alligator, sound asleep, curled on the muddy bank. He yawns and hisses at us as we glide closer to take a photo, but makes no move to vacate. Other smaller gators slide quickly into the water as we pass. We've been warned that these reptiles are so accustomed to canoeists that they have no fear and could be dangerous. We don't stick around to question that bit of advice.

Withlacoochee River

Shortly afterwards, the stream broadens. "The Juniper Prairie Wilderness," as this particular section is called, offers idyllic paddling from here on. A lone eagle soaring overhead as we approach the low bridge that marks the end of our trip provides a glorious finish to one of the most challenging and enjoyable excursions we've ever experienced . . . seven miles of sheer pleasure. It's taken us about four hours to paddle, but if you have the time, make it an all-day event. We do have to pull our canoe out of the water when we reach our destination, but we offer the driver a tip for helping us load it on his van before we return to the office to deliver our gear and claim our refund. It's well worth the extra effort. Just remember to "Pack it in, pack it out, please," as requested. And you can't get lost on this waterway as it twists along mile after mile—just go with the current's obvious flow.

GENERAL RATING: XXXX
DIFFICULTY: DIFFICULT (NOT RECOMMENDED FOR SENIORS WITH A LOW FITNESS RATING, OR SMALL CHILDREN)
SCENERY: BREATHTAKING

Withlacoochee River

PART III

SOUTHERN PENINSULA

116

THE EVERGLADES

No book proclaiming Florida's waterways would be complete without a journey into the Everglades. Touted by brochures as "a world apart," and declared an International Biosphere Preserve and a World Heritage site, the Everglades is one of the true wilderness areas left to man. Sprawling across 1.5 million acres of salt marshes, sawgrass prairies, mangroves, and lush forests, the subtropical Everglades is a vast sheet of water, the ebbs and tides of which are barely perceptible as it flows gently south some hundred miles from Lake Okeechobee into Florida Bay. The Everglades is situated in Southwest Florida, southeast of Naples and west of Miami. Commonly referred to as "the last frontier," it was aptly christened "river of grass" in 1940 by its eternal champion and pioneer conservationist, the legendary Marjory Stoneman Douglas. This wondrous ecosystem, scientists inform us, first surfaced during the Ice Age. The plain of rounded limestone covered with peat soils that lies beneath the park land was formed from the sediment of some early sea. With a maximum elevation of only 8 feet, the Everglades is home to all kinds of wildlife, including endangered species like the Florida crocodile and panther. If you're vigilant, you can also spot the elusive Everglades kite, reddish egret, roseate spoonbill, Florida mangrove cuckoo, and the Everglades mink. The death of the Everglades could occur, publications warn, mainly because of the network of manmade canals and levee systems, indiscriminately created by the misdirected U.S Army Corps of Engineers, which shuts off the life-giving bounty of rain before it can reach the national park. Because of this, natural habitats often remain unnourished. Although efforts are currently being made to restore the natural balance, pollutants, urbanization, industry, and agriculture continue to plague the Everglades, and its fate remains undecided.

CANOE RENTALS

KORESHAN STATE HISTORIC SITE
P.O. Box 7
Estero, FL 33928
(941) 992-0311

EVERGLADES NATIONAL PARK BOAT TOURS
P.O. Box 119
Everglades City, FL 33929
(941) 695-2591
(in FL) (800) 445-7725

FLORIDA BAY OUTFITTERS
P.O. Box 2513
Key Largo, FL 33037
(305) 451-3018

FLAMINGO LODGE MARINA AND OUTPOST RESORT
No. 1 Flamingo Lodge Highway
Flamingo, FL 33034-6798
(941) 695-3101
(305) 253-2241

NORTH AMERICAN CANOE TOURS, INC.
Everglades Outpost and Ivey House
P.O Box 5038
Everglades City, FL 33929
(941) 695-4666

COLLIER-SEMINOLE STATE PARK
Route 4, Box 848
Naples, FL 33961
(941) 394-3397

The Everglades is accessible from US 41, the old Tamiami Trail, the famous road that bisects the preserve. Too many commercial signs dot the roadside, but once launched on one of the many trails that leads into the interior, civilization is forgotten. Because there are so many available day adventures, and numerous liveries offering services, we pinpointed three day trips varying in length and difficulty, but appropriate for recreational canoeists or Pampered Paddlers.

COLLIER-SEMINOLE STATE PARK

The park lies within the Big Cypress Swamp and borders the Cape Romano/Ten Thousand Islands aquatic preserve. It is located 15 miles southeast of the Gulf Coast town of Naples on US 41, and 75 miles west of Miami on the section of US 41 known as the Tamiami Trail. One of our choices for Everglades exploring was the rather manicured 13.5-mile trip offered at this facility because it is ideal for those who prefer a leisurely, well-marked trail. In the early 1940s, the brochure states, Barron Collier, a wealthy advertising entrepreneur and pioneer developer, designed plans for a state park to cover 6,423 acres of the Everglades. Named for both Collier and the Seminole Indians who had made the area their home, the park was opened to the public in 1847. One feature of the land is an exotic-looking tropical hammock dominated by trees native to the coastal forests of the West Indies and the Yucatan. The park also contains a 4,760-acre wilderness preserve located in the mangrove swamp, the focus of its most popular canoe trip. Canoes rent for $3 an hour. You launch your own canoe, but it's aluminum and lightweight and easily slid from the level launching site into the water. Only a small number of canoes are available, so it's best to reserve one in advance.

CONCESSIONS

A popular tourist stop, the park's $3.25 entrance fee also covers the use of its picnic areas, 6.5-mile hiking trail, and a ranger-guided tour through the pine flatwoods and cypress swamp. A self-guided nature trail featuring a boardwalk system and observation platform overlooking the salt marsh is a must-see for wildlife devotees. Additional exhibits of plants and wildlife may be seen in the park's Interpretive Center. Boat tours, narrated by native captains aboard stable Coast Guard-certified vessels, are an alternative for those who don't wish to paddle, as well as fishing and shelling tours. Nineteen campsites are available, but should be prearranged. On exhibit is the giant walking dredge that once blazed a trail across the Everglades from Tampa to Miami. A concession stand near the water's edge provides sandwiches, cold beverages, snacks, T-shirts, camping supplies, ice, and gifts. Intoxicants and firearms are prohibited here, and pets, except for guide dogs, are not allowed in camping areas, the wilderness preserve, or the concession area. The park is open from 8 a.m. until sundown, 365 days a year, but it should be noted that because of stinging insects and subtropical heat during the summer months, the ideal season for this venture, as far as we're concerned, is from November to May. Paddles, cushions, and life jackets are issued at the park entrance with the payment of your fee. You are warned that the canoe must be back by 4 p.m. and gear returned to the entrance at that time, or you will be forced to pay a "search and rescue charge." Be sure to bring hats, layered clothing, and sunscreen for this trip, which is mostly unshaded, and use the restrooms before-hand because there are no discernible potty stops.

BLACKWATER RIVER

Aside from those who might experience a little difficulty in launching their own craft, we rate this is a perfect paddle for beginners of any age and physical condition. The channel at the outset is mostly straight, with a barely perceptible current even when it merges with the Blackwater River itself. Years ago, intending to paddle the entire loop through Mud Bay to Palm Bay and back, we got lost without a compass in a maze of myriad mangrove islands and sawgrass. Just as we were about to panic, we recognized an oddly shaped, gnarled, dead tree that had caught our eye on the way in, and were able to pinpoint our position at last. It's best for recreational canoeists to take the route prescribed by park officials. Today, we, too, are conservative, following the channel markers, numbered and positioned at intervals to guide us the entire way. The trips can be planned to fit your schedule. We choose a two-hour paddle to channel number 47, since we're planning to stay the night in Everglades City to visit other sections of the vast Everglades. Those who are not in a hurry can navigate the entire 13.5 miles in six to eight hours without a care. The waterway is a pretty sight as the creek narrows and meets the Blackwater, where it begins to wind provocatively. The tangled roots of the mangroves present an ever-changing shoreline pattern with bleached, skeletal fingers reaching for the dark water. On the way out, the numbers on the markers grow progressively higher, and arrows point you in the opposite direction. It's a popular trip, and there's quite a bit of traffic, including the periodic passage of guided tour boats, so we stay to the right. Relaxed and refreshed by our idyllic journey, we return to the launching site and pull the canoe back up to the water's edge. We like what the brochure says: "Take nothing but pictures . . . leave nothing but ripples."

GENERAL RATING: XX
DIFFICULTY: EASY
SCENERY: EXCELLENT

THE TURNER RIVER

From the sublime to the utmost of challenges, we drive down to Everglades City where we've been invited to spend the night at the Ivey House. A dormitory-type accommodation, it's rustic but spotlessly clean and comfortable. Two large restrooms at the end of the hall, one for men, one for women, provide double sinks and two separate stalls housing showers and commodes. The bed-and-breakfast inn is one of many in the quaint fishing village that offers havens for those who want to explore the Everglades and still enjoy their creature comforts. We appreciate the hospitality of our hostess, Sandee Dagley, and the home-cooked meal served that evening at 6:30 for an additional $10.

We learn that the first settler came to Everglades City in 1868. In 1923, while it was still only a fishing village, a man named Barron Collier began buying land in what became Collier County, and was instrumental in the construction of the Tamiami Trail. With the completion of the road project, Everglades City became one of the legendary Florida "boom towns." The original building now known as the Ivey House, where we're lodged, was erected at Port DuPont by the Collier interests for use as a recreational center for the road workers. After the 1925 hurricane, it was moved to its present site. One of the workers was Earl W. Ivey, who was in charge of the walking dredges (one of which is on display in the Collier-Seminole State Park). After the Trail opened in 1928, Collier converted the recreation hall to a boarding house, which was operated by Ivey and his wife, Agnes. In 1960, Ivey purchased the house, which changed hands at the time of his death, deteriorating at intervals until 1980 when David Harraden, owner of NORTH AMERICAN CANOE TOURS, Inc., purchased it from the Becket Academy. In 1989, he renovated it, retaining its original "company town" appearance. Rates are: November 1 to December 14, $40 per room; December 15 to March 15, $50; March 16 to April 30th, $40. The inn is open from November 1 through April 30. Reservations are advised.

CANOE RENTALS

We chose NORTH AMERICAN CANOE TOURS because David Harraden's tours originate here at the Ivey House, and we liked the structure's historical appeal. Harraden's varied canoe adventures, with an experienced naturalist to guide you, include all necessary equipment and a substantial lunch at a cost of $40 per person. The tours leave daily at 9 a.m., and return between 3 and 3:30 p.m. Or you can strike out on your own, as we did, if you feel confident enough. Other canoe liveries, equally efficient, are listed at the beginning of this chapter.

CONCESSIONS

Everglades City is a charming town with endless attractions, gift shops, inns, and restaurants including the legendary Rod and Gun Lodge, formerly a private club that often housed the rich and famous. Bike rentals, hiking trails, kayak tours, sightseeing boats, shelling, and fabulous fishing abound as well as inviting antique and gift shops. You can buy drinks here, or bring your own bottle if you prefer.

THE TRAIL

The Turner River was named after Richard B. Turner, a Seminole war scout who led a military unit up the Chokoloskee Creek in 1857, resulting in several of the closing battles of the Seminole War. Later on, Turner homesteaded on the river, and the ruins of his house can be spotted along the eastern shore. The trip is a rugged one, requiring endurance, paddling skills, and a certain amount of' athletic ability if you choose the route through the mangrove tunnels as we do. Although David spells out the pitfalls, nothing prepares us for what's in store. We're shuttled in a comfortable van to the launching site, but it's the last comfort we'll experience for the next six hours. (Note: Be sure to use the restroom before you leave, and drink only small amounts of liquids because there are no easily accessible potty-stops here.) We packed our own lunch. As David warns us, we're bravely embarking on a do-it-yourself trip. We set out jauntily and confidently ahead of our fellow passengers, who are part of the guided tour, delighting in being totally alone in our surroundings. This is what red-blooded, be it only occasional canoeists dream about . . . a remote wilderness teeming with noisy tropical birds like wood storks, herons, falcons, ibis, and varieties of migratory birds using the Everglades for wintering or stopovers. Strange rustling sounds in the thick underbrush signal unknown presences that could be panthers, maybe deer. We spot several alligators, including a scaly nine-footer, but they scramble away at our approach, some swimming ahead of us, their passage clearly discernible underwater. We paddle the mirror-like waters past the ever-present saw grass while fish of all sizes and shapes seem to accompany us. It's easy going until we reach the first of the so-called "mangrove tunnels." David has informed us that this trail is unmarked, but here, crouched Indian-style on our knees in the bottom of our canoe, reaching out at times for the mangrove roots to propel us, we see branches and tree trunks scraped raw by the countless paddles of earlier canoeists. It's a 20-minute survival test, but we struggle through to open water at last, taking deep breaths, savoring the rich aroma of sulphur and rotting vegetation. It's the second tunnel that does us in. Like the first, it seems impassable at first sight, but we've been instructed to enter the small, forbidding-looking opening. It's pure chance when we catch up with a couple in the tunnel ahead of us, the first humans we've seen for over two hours.

John raises the camera for a great shot of them laboring through the tangled undergrowth, and fails to dodge a low-hanging branch. The impact sends the canoe sideways, and before we can recover, it overturns and we're standing waist-deep in the murky water, and ankle-deep in muck. The squawking of an unseen bird sounds remarkably like derisive laughter. Fortunately, our fellow canoeists, Margaret and John Kinzer from Hilton Head, are able to help salvage our gear, jackets, ice chest, and my notes, but the camera and the photos of our last two trips are lost forever. John and I manage to hoist our traitorous vessel to a nest of branches, turn it over to drain the water, then right it once again. With the help of the Kinzers, we reload our canoe, and, subdued, continue on our way. It's the first time in twenty years we've tipped over, which proves that in a canoe, as on a highway, you can't be distracted by anything. The journey seems easy after that, and even though we're soaked, the day is balmy and we're not chilled. As we reach another broad expanse of the lake, the sight of three manatees rolling alongshore cheers us to some degree. The final tunnel confronting us is easy compared to the last two, and once we're through and reach Turner Lake with its power boats and the river homes lining the banks, we're back to civilization and on the last leg. It's been a tough six hours, and we're tired and aching, and we mourn the loss of our camera, but still feel it's all been worth it. Our car is parked at the general store which is David's headquarters, but we head for the Ivey House to shower and change before driving back to Sarasota.

GENERAL RATING: XXXX
DIFFICULTY: DEFINITELY DIFFICULT
SCENERY: OUTSTANDING
NOTE: If we've discouraged you from taking this trip, you can let David shuttle you to another launch site for what is known as the Hatchet Creek trip, a shorter and far easier excursion involving none of the mangrove tunnels, but including the beautiful vistas of saw grass prairies, mangrove wilderness, and several areas of higher ground richly vegetated with tall pines and gnarled oaks. There are innumerable trips available at the other listed liveries, but the area is vast and many of the trips similar in nature. We have selected those we feel best acquaint you with the many ever-changing faces of the wondrous Everglades.

Turner River

BRADEN RIVER

Located in Manatee County in west-central Florida on the Gulf Coast, the river begins its course in a central Manatee County watershed and flows for about 25 miles until it merges with the Manatee River. From I-75, take exit 41 (SR 70), and travel west toward Bradenton for 1.5 miles to the intersection with Braden River Road.

The Braden River has a long history, going back to 1539 when Hernando de Soto landed there and made a pact with the peaceful Timucuan Indians at the site of an ancient village now known as Madira Bickel Mound. The De Soto Pageant, commemorating this event, is still a popular annual attraction. Its present name was derived from a wealthy sugar plantation owner named Dr. Joseph Braden, who farmed and developed the land in the area during the civil war. "Bradentown," as it was called before the name was shortened to Bradenton, occupied a favorable location at the confluence of the Braden and Manatee rivers, and for a time was one of the most important settlements on the Gulf Coast. River traffic was once heavy with shipments of sugar products, citrus, and cattle.

CANOE RENTALS

JIGG'S LANDING
6106 Braden River Road
Bradenton, FL
(941) 756-6745
Ray Caurson

Jigg's Landing, located between Bradenton and Sarasota on SR 70 off I-75, is not one of your better known embarkation points in Suthwest Florida, but offers friendly cracker-style service. The area is familiar to a few avid fisherfolk and locals who know a good thing but prefer to keep it to themselves. It's easy launching from the dock there, and you can rent a good, steady aluminum canoe for a straight fee of $18. There are a limited number of canoes, so reservations are a good idea, especially weekends. Try this trip during the cooler weather, because paddling across the wide expanse of lake to get to the scenic part of the excursion can be a hot and tiring experience. And there's the trip back to consider, even though there's no current to impede you. By the time this goes to press, Ray assures me back rests will be available.

CONCESSIONS

There's a small but well-stocked convenience store to provide you with fishing tackle, bait, ice, soft drinks, hamburgers, snacks, and other supplies. Restrooms with running water are located outside the store. It's definitely primitive, but picturesque, with cottages for rent if you want to stay overnight and don't mind roughing it. There's even a pool table if you find some extra time on your hands. You can chat with the amiable locals who will give you fishing tips and confirm that the fishing is excellent. But it's Linger Lodge that's the real attraction. About five miles further on, it should take about two hours to paddle. The lodge's pavilion is a real treat, with a wooden deck overlooking the river and umbrella-shaded tables. Inside, you'll find the legendary rattlesnake bar with rattler hides laminated into the wood . . . skins of snakes that owner Frank Gamsky killed while clearing his land 22 years ago. There's a pool table there, too, if you want a change of pace. The menu includes fresh fish, chicken, and gator, served any way you like it, soft drinks, and cold beer. It's southern hospitality at its best. Gamsky, a self-taught taxidermist, has made a museum of the place with displays of stuffed animals, birds, and a magnificent collection of rattlesnake skins as well as arrowheads and fossils. If you get a chance to talk to Frank, he has some tall tales to tell.

THE TRAIL

The Braden River is unique in that it's one of the Florida rivers that flow north. Part of it is fresh water, part brackish. This is a round trip (roughly, four hours), so figure on two hours more or less, depending on your strength and skill, to paddle to Linger Lodge, which is well worth the effort and provides a welcome respite. After we cross the wide expanse of Ward Lake, the trail narrows to a scenic waterway called Rattlesnake Slough, lined with bearded oaks, palms and mangroves. Even on a Saturday morning, it's so quiet we can hear the hum of busy insects in the brush. There's plenty of wildlife, all kinds of birds and turtles, and gators.

The occasional small power boat courteously slows as it passes. We suggest you layer clothing for comfort, keeping cool breezes off the water in mind, and shed as you go along. Winter months are best . . . no bugs, no sweat. There are several inviting spots along the way where we pull up and stretch our legs. We're abruptly aware of civilization when we pass under Linger Lodge Road with its steady roar of traffic, but when we reach Linger Lodge we're back in old Florida. After we've rested, we paddle a little farther on past the Lodge and a small cluster of homes to where the river narrows even more, and each twisting turn reveals one breathtaking vista after the other. It's decidedly more scenic here. But there's the homeward excursion to face. It's important that we Pampered Paddlers pace ourselves.

GENERAL RATING: XX
SCENERY: FAIR
DIFFICULTY: EASY . . . EXCEPT FOR SOME STRENUOUS
PADDLING ACROSS THE LAKE.

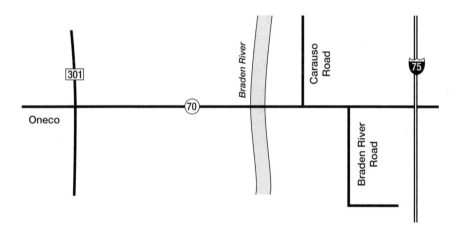

ESTERO RIVER

T his designated canoe trail is located on the Gulf Coast, in Lee County, near the Koreshan State Historic Site, ten miles south of Fort Meyers. "Estero" is a Spanish word meaning "estuary," a small river into which the tide flows. Around the turn of the century, pioneer families From Portugal, Spain, and Scotland arrived in Punta Gorda by railway from Chicago. From there, they traveled by boat down the Peace River, Caloosahatchee River, Matanzas Pass, the Gulf of Mexico, along Estero Island, and into Estero Bay and the river. For many years, the Estero River remained the "highway to the world" because it was so accessible to many connecting waterways. Today, commercial fishing, the citrus industry, and the tourist trade keep the area alive as a popular destination resort. The Koreshan Settlement (its name derived from "Koresh," the Hebrew word for Cyrus), was established over a hundred years ago by pioneers from New York State, Illinois, and California . . . 200 devout people who believed in communal living, communal ownership of property, and celibacy. Their unique religion included the belief that the earth was a hollow sphere in which life existed on the outer surface, overlooking the sun, stars and universe in its core. The people followed their leader south to the banks of the Estero River to carve the New Jerusalem out of the Florida wilderness. The carefully preserved settlement is worth seeing, and the park itself is beautifully maintained.

CANOE RENTALS

THE KORESHAN STATE HISTORIC SITE
US 41 at Corkscrew Road
P.O. Box 7
Estero FL 33928
(941) 992-0311

TACKLE AND CANOE OUTFITTERS
20991 South Tamiami Trail
Estero, FL 33928
(941) 992-4050

Take Exit 19 off I-75, then travel west on Corkscrew Road for two miles to US 41 or Tamiami Trail. Turn right (north) and continue for one-quarter mile to the bridge over the Estero River to the CANOE OUTFITTERS, located on the northeast side of the bridge. The KORESHAN STATE PARK CANOE OUTFITTERS, managed by Larry Fooks, is located in the Park itself.

Paula Stuller and her family have been renting and selling canoes at the CANOE OUTFITTERS since 1977. They offer a four-and-a-half-hour trip that is both recreational and relaxing for the experienced canoeist as well as the novice. You can enjoy a leisurely all-day paddle in a comfortable Mohawk canoe down the picturesque Estero River for $17.50. Back rests are available, and cushions and life jackets are provided. It's an easy launch, with able assistance, from a small wooden dock.

The livery is open from 7 a.m. until sunset, seven days a week. Larry Fooks' operation in the park is open daily from 8 a.m. until 2 hours before sunset. The livery has 18 canoes available at $3 per hour or $15 per day.

CONCESSIONS

The CANOE OUTFITTERS OUTPOST offers snacks, fresh and saltwater bait and tackle, and even a complete taxidermy service along with the obligatory restrooms. The managers are friendly, and provide maps pinpointing the Koreshan State Historic Site should you decide to stop and explore it. It's open from 8 a.m. until sunset, with picnic facilities, nature trails, an a museum. If you're the sporting type, you can camp overnight there after making the necessary arrangements.

THE TRAIL

Because of the powerboat traffic on weekends, we recommend you make this a weekday trip. If you elect to rent from the Stullers, the journey, which ultimately leads to Estero Bay, takes you past land that has been preserved in its natural state. Its water is spring-fed tidal water, saltier as you go west, fresher toward the east. After we paddle about a mile in a westerly direction under the US 41 bridge, enjoying the breeze from the bay, we pass the Koreshan State Park, and several buildings of the settlement can be seen through the woods to the left. We picnic here and make a "potty stop." Both trips take us past trailer parks scarcely visible through the screen of giant, moss-draped oaks with their clinging bromeliads, and from that point on, the scenery is excellent. The banks are lined with moss-covered limestone outcropping and lush vegetation including mangroves, turtle grass, spartina grass, varieties of colorful hibiscus and other wildflowers. Tall Australian and sand pines stand guard on the higher ground. Alligators and turtles sun themselves on partly submerged logs in the murky, tannin-stained waters; busy otters paddle back and forth near their hidden holes. It is the habitat of every variety of bird including the graceful osprey, and we spot a lone eagle's nest and the hull of a sunken boat. Fish are abundant, and stingrays and horseshoe crabs scuttle across the sandy bottoms near the mangrove islands. Tall river grasses signal the widening of the river to approximately 50 feet at intervals, and when we reach a picturesque little waterway appropriately called Halfway Creek, we explore some of the many provocative channels that weave in and out through mangroves and turtle grass. We've brought our compass along on this trip (always a good idea), because it's easy for weekend canoeists like ourselves to get confused if we stray from the main course. One basic rule we've learned is to "go with the flow" . . . of the current, that is. In all, it's one of the most pleasant and navigable waterways in the south of Florida.

GENERAL RATING: XXXX
DIFFICULTY: EASY
SCENERY: EXCELLENT

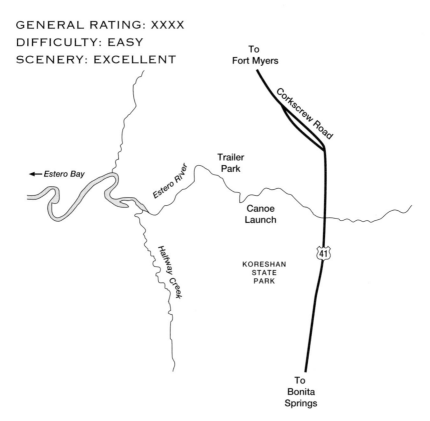

FLORIDA KEYS
JOHN PENNEKAMP CORAL REEF STATE PARK

There is an entrance fee to the park of $4.25 for 2 people; $5.25 for four people; 50 cents each additional passenger. Located at Mile Marker 102.5, north of Key Largo in Monroe County, only an hour south of Miami, the first underwater state park in the country covers approximately 70 nautical square miles of coral reefs, seagrass beds, and mangrove swamps. The park areas, thankfully, were designed to protect and preserve the only remaining live coral reef of the continental United States. It lies about six miles offshore and parallels the Florida Keys. Coral reefs, for the uninitiated, are composites of skeletal remains of corals, and remains of other plant and animal life bonded into masses by limestone secretions and calcareous algae. The park also contains, as various government pamphlets inform us, 53,661 acres of submerged land and 2,350 acres of uplands. The seagrass meadows found in the waters of the park provide valuable nursery areas, feeding grounds, and shelter for many varieties of marine life. Even the decaying seagrass has a function here. Mixed with other organic debris, we're told, it becomes a substance used as food for much of the microscopic life that exists beneath the water's surface. The seagrass community of this vast park system is an important buffer between the coral reef and the islands that form the populated Florida Keys. It traps sediments, excessive amounts of which, if settled on the live coral, reduce the supply of food and sunlight.

CANOE RENTALS

CORAL REEF PARK COMPANY, INC.
P.O. Box 1560
Key Largo, FL 33037
(305) 451-1202

LONG KEY STATE RECREATION AREA
P.O. Box 776
Long Key, FL 33001
(305) 664-4815

BISCAYNE NATIONAL UNDERWATER PARK
8755 SW 328th Street,
P.O. Box 1270
Homestead, FL 33030

NOTE: These rentals embark from different points for viewing the keys, but all trips are similar in nature. Some of the liveries in the Everglades also service the area. We recommend that you make reservations for any trip you decide to take, and, preferably, on a weekday. The concessions were mobbed on the idyllic Sunday in February we chose to explore the keys. We were lucky enough to rent the last canoe at 2 p.m. Others had to take numbers and wait in line for the privilege. Canoes rent for $8 an hour; $28 half-day; $48 all-day. Kayaks are also available. The service is great. After checking in at the office, you collect your gear at the supply area near the water's edge, you are given instructions, and your canoe is readied by willing attendants. A laminated, waterproof map is handily attached and dangles before you at either end of the canoe. There's no way you can get lost here, because all channels eventually head you to your destination. Be sure to bring sunscreen and a hat for this one, and wear shorts as there are no shaded areas. It was 85 degrees out there, and it was hot. You have your choice of any length trip, depending on how much time you have and how many byways you elect to explore, from 20 minutes to 2 hours or more. There are no back rests. And no potty-stops, so keep that in mind when you start out.

CONCESSIONS

Besides a separate, modern, well-maintained bathhouse with showers, changing rooms, and toilet stalls, the park manages a well-stocked gift and souvenir shop. You can buy quality souvenirs, gifts, and clothing (even bathing suits), books describing the area, or merely browse. Snacks, fishing supplies, snorkeling and diving gear, fast food, soft drinks . . . it's all here. It's a mecca for those who love snorkeling, scuba diving, fishing, sailing, swimming in crystal-clear temperate waters, or viewing the wonderland below from glass-bottomed boats that leave at intervals. There's a campground with excellent facilities.

THE TRAIL

Although the many varieties of mangroves lining the water's edge are attractive and create interesting root patterns, they are predictable. The big attraction here lies in the plant and marine life underwater. After a few hundred yards of easy paddling, we turn off the main course into a picturesque narrow channel where motor traffic is prohibited. Here, kayaks and canoes vie for position, some of the more inexperienced unable to successfully navigate the turns and getting hopelessly entangled in the mangrove roots. It reminds us of our own initial canoe trips. After we paddle safely past them, we study the many species of plants flowing beneath the water . . . the manatee grass, turtle grass, shoal grass, and widgeon grass. Our close observation of the river bottom recalls the little ditty that helps boaters, including canoeists, use the color of the water to determine its depth:

Brown, brown, run aground;
Green, green, nice and clean;
White, white, you just might;
Blue, blue, sail on through.

Schools of parrotfish, surgeonfish, and mangrove snapper swim in the underwater meadows, and we see stingrays scuttling across the sandy bottom, sea stars, small crabs, and queen conches. There's too much traffic today, unfortunately, to spot the shy manatees, sea turtles, or alligators, but we know they're prudently hiding out until the visitors depart. There are the usual number of wading birds including the roseate spoonbill, white ibis, and reddish egret. Even though there's no challenge here, it's pleasurable and worthwhile, an ideal novice paddle.

GENERAL RATING: XX
DIFFICULTY: VERY EASY
SCENERY: FAIR

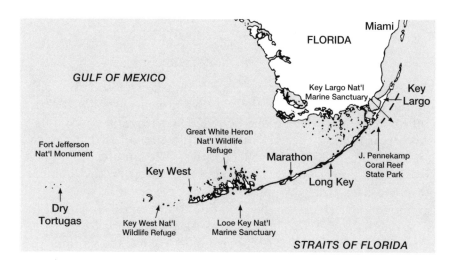

33. LOXAHATCHEE RIVER

The only Florida river designated as a National Wild and Scenic River, a recognition given in 1985, the eight-mile-long Loxahatchee is a paddler's paradise. It is located in Martin and Palm Beach counties. Loxahatchee means "river of turtles," so described by early Indians presumably because it is home to countless colonies of the reptiles. The greater part of the river flows through the Jonathan Dickinson State Park, which has a history of its own. We're informed that a Quaker merchant named Jonathan Dickinson, and his family, were shipwrecked in 1696 off the coast in the Hobe Sound area. The Dickinsons and other survivors made their torturous way up the coast to St. Augustine, and many of their trials and encounters with Native Americans and Spanish settlers are described in Dickinson's journals. The 11,500 acres of land that comprise the Jonathan Dickinson State Park are named after this early pioneer family. The park was headquarters for the Signal Corps during World War II, then was transfered to the state of Florida for public use in 1950. Two of the original Army buildings are still present.

CANOE RENTALS

JONATHAN DICKINSON STATE PARK
16450 SE Federal Highway
Hobe Sound, FL 33455
(407) 546-2771

CANOE OUTFITTERS
16346 106th Terrace North
Jupiter, FL 33478
(407) 746-7053

To get to Jonathan Dickinson State Park, take I-95 and exit on SR 706; drive east to Federal Highway (US 1); then travel north about eight miles to the park in Hobe Sound. The park is open seven days a week year-round. There is an entrance fee of $3.25 per vehicle, which includes full use of the facilities. The number of canoes allowed on the river each day is limited to protect the environment, so call ahead to avoid disappointment or time spent in waiting . . . also phone to check on weather and tide conditions. Canoes rent for $6 for one hour; $10 for 2 hours; $13 for three hours; $16 for four hours; $18 for five hours; $20 for six hours. We feel the six-hour trip is long enough for more conservative paddlers, but there are rates for additional hours. Canoes must be returned by 5 p.m, and swimming is prohibited. This is one of those state park do-it-yourself excursions, and you are responsible for hauling the canoe off the dock and sliding it into the water, also for returning it to its original storage site. For this reason, park rentals are not recommended for those not able to handle this kind of physical exertion. Some may wish to rely on the kindness of strangers. We helped a woman and her young children lift their canoe out of the water, upend it, and place it alongside the others. Fortunately, the canoes are small and lightweight. As of this writing they're a bit battered, but they're easy to maneuver, and, most importantly, watertight. Unlike some we've rented, they remained dry throughout the trip.

For those who want to be pampered and don't mind paying a little extra, the CANOE OUTFITTERS, operating since 1980, provide more personalized service including shuttles to embarkation points and pickups. Kayaks can also be rented, and instruction for each type of craft is available. They are open Wednesday through Sunday, 8 a.m. to 5 p.m.; closed Easter Day, Thanksgiving Day; Christmas Day, and New Year's Day. Call ahead to make reservations. Guided paddling trips include information about the river. The two solo adventure trips are:

Trip #1: 5–6 hours of paddling approximately eight miles. It begins at 11:30 a.m., and return transportation is arranged, varying according to schedules. The cost is $25 for two people.

Trip #2: $6 for the first hour, $4 for each additional hour, arranged according to the wishes of the paddler.

CONCESSIONS

The office, located in the general store in JONATHAN DICKINSON STATE PARK, rents out canoes and also cabins. It sells souvenirs, T-shirts, cold drinks, ice, snacks, sandwiches, and camping supplies. It is open seven days a week, the same hours as the park itself. There are pleasant picnic areas, and clean, modern restrooms located in the bathhouse. But there is no swimming, and canoeists are asked not to leave their canoes except at Trapper Nelson's, one of the area's main attractions. A loner, young Nelson came to live in a cabin on a high bank next to the river. For 38 years he lived off the land, and locals dubbed him the "wild man of the Loxahatchee." In spite of his limited education, he made enough money trapping and selling furs to amass many acres of land, and built a wildlife zoo, additional log cabins, lush tropical gardens, and a Seminole Indian "Chickee" shelter. His little estate became a tourist attraction. After his death in 1968, the state acquired his land, preserving his home and grounds. At that time, the animals were released and all that remain are empty cages, but it's nice to pull up to the old rustic dock, walk the grounds, and have a picnic. The site is open 9 a.m. to 5 p.m., and when you arrive you're greeted by one of the ranger guides, every day except Monday and Tuesday. Cold drinks are sold there. The Park also offers guided tours aboard the 44-passenger Loxahatchee Queen II.

THE TRAIL

The moment we begin this journey that originates in the park, we're struck by its spectacular beauty and loneliness. The river is wide, winding through mangrove swamps at this point, its sandy bluffs lined with sand pine scrub and pine flatwoods, storm-cropped palms, and silvery, skeletal trunks of once-proud old bald cypress trees. Numerous osprey nests are evident in the upper-most branches, and we spot several osprey soaring overhead. Colonies of turtles bask in the sun on every available projection. After thirty minutes of vigorous paddling against the current, we venture into Kitching Creek, a narrow, winding bittersweet-chocolate stream. Here, the water's surface is still and glassy, and the silence unbroken except for the call of birds. Don't miss this little side trip . . . a jungle of tangled vines, river grass, and snarls of mangroves. Rustlings in the undergrowth are evidence of unseen creatures, and we spy a young alligator easing itself into the murky depths of the water as we approach. An exotic green heron with iridescent feathers lifts its head as we pass, then continues its vigil at the water's edge. Once back on the river, we find it becomes narrower as it snakes its way through the wilderness, then widens once more. Venturing closer to shore, we spot a giant gator, half-hidden and motionless amid the ferns and saw grass and tangled branches. It's a beautiful Monday in March, and except for an occasional fisherman, there's little sign of humans until the big tour boat laden with passengers overtakes us with its loudspeaker, and the silence is broken. We tie up at

Trader Nelson's, and although it's closed today, we peer in at the empty cages and the buildings, and picnic on the sagging old dock. There's a larger picnic area about 40 minutes further on, and a beautiful cypress swamp on the upper river. We've been told there's an Indian mound up ahead, and a concrete dam with a drop of about two feet as you skim over it. We'd like to try it sometime, but we've run out of time exploring the little byways, so we head back, paddling at a more leisurely pace with the current. The scenery is just as splendid from this direction, and we're struck anew by the pristine and ever-changing beauty of the Loxahatchee. Otter, raccoons, deer, and even bobcats can be spotted on the shore if you're lucky. Once back at the park, we manage to haul our canoe back into place with little difficulty, but, again, remind anyone who isn't in good physical shape not to try this trip. We've spent five hours paddling steadily, at times

Loxahatchee River

vigorously, on the broad, windswept portions of the river. It's not an easy paddle for the pampered.

GENERAL RATING: XXXX
DIFFICULTY: MODERATE TO STRENUOUS
SCENERY: SPECTACULAR

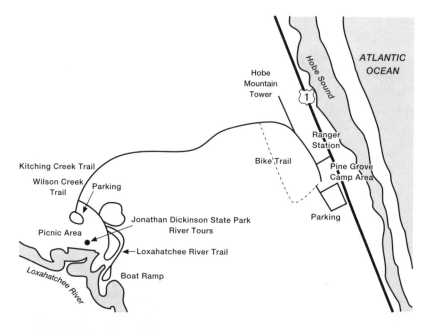

Loxahatchee River

LITTLE MANATEE RIVER

B eginning as a twisting creek in a swampy area east of Fort Lone-some in Southeastern Hillsborough County, the Manatee River flows about 40 miles before broadening and emptying into Tampa Bay. Calusa and Timucuan Native Americans called the river, which divided the two tribes, the "Singing River" because legends told of the beautiful music it mysteriously made on certain moonlit nights. This part of the river is located near Rye, a community which no longer exists and which was the site of the first railroad bridge, built in 1880, to transport the old Orange Blossom Special. Rye was named after one of its early settlers, a Scotsman named Erasmus Rye. The waterway was once the main route to the interior for the area's first settlers, supply-ing a steamboat service from Braidenton (another early spelling) to Rye. The land was used for cattle grazing, farming, and harvesting lumber. Because of its unspoiled beauty, it has been designated as an "Outstanding Florida Water" and has the purest water quality in the state despite being stained a rusty color by decaying vegetation.

CANOE RENTALS

CANOE OUTPOST, Wilderness Canoe Adventures
18001 U.S. 301 North
Wimauma, FL 33598
(813) 634-2228

Take I-75 North, Exit 43 to 301 North. Head north until you reach the Little Manatee River. The outpost, one of Florida's oldest and largest canoe outfitters, is located on the southwest side of the river, and is open six days a week, 8 a.m. to 5 p.m., closed on Tues-day. Rentals are $25 per canoe for a day trip for two people. Third parties under 14 years of age are free; all others are charged an addi-tional $5. Canoes are aluminum, clean, and roomy. Back rests are available for $1. The friendly owners, Frank and Jan Lapniewski, give detailed descriptions of trail options for the downstream float trips. We elected Trip 3, the easy section, which is approximately 2 hours paddle time to the Little Manatee River State Park, with an optional additional three-and-a-half mile loop to cover a total of ten miles and an additional two hours. The bus takes you upriver every hour beginning at 9:30 a.m. You can leave the Outpost as late as noon for this one. The other two trails include leisurely nine-mile and sixteen-mile trips on the upper section with similar scenery. Pick-ups at the end of the excursion are at the designated spot every hour.

CONCESSIONS

The Canoe Outpost is a small, rustic building that offers only soft drinks, so bring your own picnic lunch. And kindly take your trash back with you. The river is kept reasonably free of debris by the Canoe Outpost's staff, with the help of several regular canoeists. The restrooms are clean and modern. Personally, we don't advise swimming in the murky waters, a possible haven for stray gators. The Little Manatee State Recreation Area, covering about 1,600 acres on the south shore west of US 301, at which you can stop on the way, offers picnic tables, camping, a 6.5-mile nature trail along the river, fishing (license required), and horse trails for those who own their own horses.

THE TRAIL

The launch site is rough, but Frank is there, husky and capable, and you do little more than hoist up one end of the canoe and carry the gear down the steep hill. Once underway, it's hard to believe such a pristine and primitive waterway exists only an hour from the heart of Sarasota. We paddle the Little Manatee on a Saturday morning in October and are surprised to encounter only an occasional canoeist. It's said this is the wildest section of the river and the most difficult to paddle when there's high water. We learned that the hard way when we chose to try the upstream section (east of US 301) one morning after heavy rains, and were propelled too rapidly through all kinds of snags, and caught up against fallen trees. At times, we had to lie back and help snake the canoe under fallen trees with our hands because of the high water. But today, in the downstream area, it's a piece of cake! The current isn't too swift, the masses of tangled foliage have been cleared, and it's easy to glide under the obstacles and beneath the overhanging branches. The steep, sandy banks on either side of the narrow, twisting trail give us the feeling of being isolated from the rest of the world. Only the chorus of unseen insects and the calls of wading birds interrupt the stillness. We find ourselves speaking in whispers to avoid disturbing colonies of drowsing turtles, and once we pass breathlessly within a few feet of a young alligator napping on a muddy bank. "Big Mama," lurking in the reeds nearby, bellows an eerie but unmistakable warning as we glide by. Later on, a more adventurous gator slips quietly past our canoe and sinks into the murky depths. The sighting of an eagle perched high on the branches of a dead tree is the highlight of the day. About 4.5 miles out you encounter one of the few signs of civilization: the looming concrete walls of the Florida Intake Plant. The twists and turns of the Little Manatee require a little extra skill, but the trip is leisurely, the gentle movement of the current at your back giving the illusion of swift paddling. And everywhere, the bearded oaks, sand palms, and a variety of wildflowers! The last little jog through the winding, remote bayous winds up one of the most pleasurable trips we've ever taken. This is the real Florida . . . a virtually unspoiled, wilderness splendor.

GENERAL RATING: XXXX
DIFFICULTY: MODERATE, DIFFICULT AFTER HEAVY RAINS
SCENERY: EXCELLENT

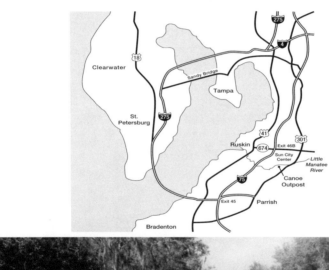

Little Manatee

OTHER ADVENTURES

It's worth noting here that the Canoe Outpost, Wilderness Canoe Adventures, also offers a pleasant excursion on Cockroach Bay, the last healthy estuary left on Tampa Bay. This trip is available by appointment only, from November to March. The cost is $20 per person. Frank shuttles us over to the Bay and guides us through this hundred-island maze where mangroves, saltmarshes, seagrass meadows, mud flats, and oyster beds are key elements and fascinating to explore. Scientists call this estuary "the cradle of the ocean" because it's a "prime breeding, feeding, and hiding place" for myriad sea creatures. At Frank's signal, we stop at several little islands along the way to seine the bottom and unearth some of the sea life, marveling over them before we return them to their undersea homes. The bay is a haven for all kinds of wildlife, and a must for bird watchers. Pelicans, egrets, roseate spoonbills, and varieties of herons are among those that can be spotted. Any nature enthusiast will thrill at a chance to venture into an ecosystem that is fast disappearing.

GENERAL RATING: XX
DIFFICULTY: EASY
SCENERY: FAIR

UPPER MANATEE RIVER

There are many sections of this long, winding river on the Gulf Coast in Manatee County, but the Upper Manatee, as it's sometimes called, deserves special attention. It's only about an hour from Bradenton Gulf Beaches, St. Petersburg, Sarasota, or Tampa. Because of its unspoiled beauty and importance as a vital natural resource, the upper reach of the river has been designated as a State Canoe Trail and Greenway, ensuring its preservation for future generations.

CANOE RENTALS

RAY'S CANOE HIDEAWAY
1247 Hagle Park Road
Bradenton, FL 34202
(941) 747-3909

AQUATEL RESORT
4315 Aquatel Road
Bradenton, FL 34202
(941) 746-6884

To get to RAY'S CANOE HIDEAWAY, a facility that intrigued us because of its name, take I-75 and travel toward Bradenton. Exit on 42 A or B, and go east about 2.5 miles on SR 64. Turn left (north) on Upper Manatee Road (toward Christian Retreat) and proceed about 4.5 miles to Hagle Park Road. Turn north and follow the signs to RAY'S CANOE HIDEAWAY. Ray has been operating the facility quietly and efficiently for the past four years. He offers a choice of 50 battered and bruised fiberglass or aluminum canoes, but they're watertight and serviceable. It's an easy launch from the gently sloping ramp, and he helps us settle into our craft, hands us cushions, life jackets, paddles, and a whistle for emergencies, then gives us a map of the river highlighting several landmarks. Ray's is open 8 a.m. until sunset, every day except Tuesday and Wednesday. His prices are reasonable: half-day (up to 5 hours) $6 per person, full day (5–12 hours) $9 per person. If you care to spend the night in the wilderness among unknown creatures, you can try it for $13 per person.

CONCESSIONS

RAY'S CANOE HIDEAWAY is aptly named because only a few enthusiastic paddlers know of its existence. It's a first for us. He makes no pretense at being a fancy concession with his rustic office, but does have a supply of bait, tackle, rental fishing gear, cold drinks, snacks, candy, and ice. What more do you need? As usual, to play it safe, we brought our cooler along with our own nourishing lunch.

THE TRAIL

This is a serene and easily navigable section of the river even though there is shallow water in some sections on this beautiful November morning. Today, it takes a watchful eye and some careful maneuvering to avoid the many sandbars. (Ray has assured us the water in the Manatee is seldom this low). Paddling upstream against a practically non-existent current, we cautiously seek out the darker-hued channels of the coffee-colored water, which in spite of its murky look, is mostly pure. It's a wonderfully scenic and quiet paddle with steep, heavily foliaged sandy banks rising on either side. Gnarled bearded oaks, cedars, and sandpalms with their usual blankets of vines and wildflowers give it a jungly look. Easily accessible stretches of white sand offer inviting spots to stretch our legs and explore the shallows. Small clams, coquinas, and other varieties of shells dot the beaches, and we see the tracks of a giant wading bird disappearing into the undergrowth. We spot many varieties of graceful birds, turtles, and, to our delight, a seven-foot gator, half-sub-

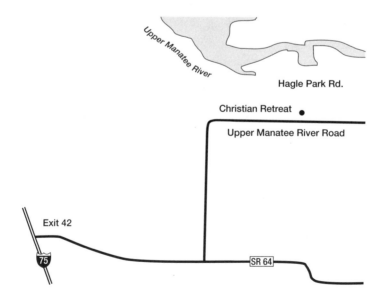

merged in the water near the bank. We're told manatees frequent these waters during the warmer weather, but are disappointed by their absence today. We pass the remains of the old railroad bridge that once spanned the river, and a little farther up ahead, there's a swimming hole complete with a rope for swinging out over the water and jumping in over the formations of limestone outcroppings that line the banks. We choose to picnic here on a sandy beach, enjoying our noise-free interlude. It's a halfway mark for us, about an hour-and-a-half paddle, and after venturing a little further where the river seems to grow even more dangerously shallow (we have no desire to portage), we start back downstream, resting now and then and allowing the gentle flow to carry us. You can make this an approximate four-hour, easy paddle. It's ideal for just soaking up the silence, meditating, and enjoying the unspoiled wilderness of the Manatee.

GENERAL RATING: XX
DIFFICULTY: MODERATE
SCENERY: EXCELLENT

Upper Manatee River

MYAKKA RIVER
SNOOK HAVEN, CURRY CREEK (SOUTH), AND MYAKKA RIVER STATE PARK

The river, which many insist is the most beautiful in Florida, is over 65 miles long, beginning as a trickle of water in the pastures of eastern Manatee County, and petering out in Charlotte County. The Indians named it Myakka, meaning "big water." It is designated as "wild and scenic," and is pleasantly canoeable, we feel, only for the portion that flows for 34 miles through Sarasota County. But from origin to end, the Myakka has been less disturbed than any other river in the area. While larger and more navigable rivers were being densely settled or mined for phosphate, the slower and shallower waters of the Myakka have been spared commercial intrusion. The river and its banks and surrounding marshland are home to an enormous alligator population as well as white-tailed deer, wild hogs, and turkeys. Many game fish abound, including an occasional shark or tarpon. In the past, native Floridians fashioned rafts of buoyant palmetto logs and floated salt pork and produce down river to meet the boats at Punta Gorda. The lower section of the river, which we traveled first, is accessible in Venice just off US 41.

CANOE RENTAL (SOUTH, CURRY CREEK)

SNOOK HAVEN FISH CAMP
5000 East Venice Avenue
Venice, FL 34292
(941) 485-7221

CANOE RENTAL (NORTH)

MYAKKA RIVER STATE PARK
13207 SR 72
Sarasota, FL 34241-9542
(941) 361-6511

The launching site of the southern part of the Myakka is located in Venice, and is called SNOOK HAVEN. If you're traveling south on I-75, take Exit 34 and turn south on River Road. At Venice Avenue, turn east and follow the signs—and a bumpy dirt road—to Snook Haven. The canoes are a bit battered, but they're serviceable. Rental fees are $12 for 2 hours, $15 for 3 hours, $25 for all day. The

3-hour trip covers approximately 6–7 miles. You're transported to a launching site at Curry Creek. From there you paddle to the Myakka River, continue for a mile or so, then head back to Snook Haven, an easy trip, and scenic for the most part. You can decide how long a trip you desire. Weekdays are best if you don't like crowds. Most of the time, the trail is kept free of litter, but there was still enough bobbing around or caught on the banks to upset us. The Myakka State Park, 14 miles east on SR 72, which offers an entirely different type of excursion, is better policed, and the wildlife on its 45 square miles is closely guarded, regulations strictly enforced. There is a $3.25 entrance fee, which covers up to 8 occupants of your car. Canoes are launched at the edge of Myakka Lake and cost $10 for 2 hours; $18 for 3 hours; $25 for 5 or more hours.

CONCESSIONS

The SNOOK HAVEN facility includes a lodge and a popular restaurant, and a bar that dates back to the early part of the century. SNOOK HAVEN has a colorful history of wild parties, free-for-alls, and horse-racing along the river. The owners have spruced up the place but have retained the rustic ambiance. You can still get a game of pool, enjoy one of the weekly barbecues with stompin' music on the outdoor bandstand, or sit on the wooden deck overlooking the water and order down-home country food like chicken, ribs, fried catfish or shrimp, or beer or wine from the bar.

MYAKKA RIVER STATE PARK has a well-stocked concession stand with snacks, soft drinks, fishing supplies, and souvenirs. You may choose to eat on the premises or take a picnic lunch, but be advised, the "no littering" laws are enforced. An airboat tour is available, on which a seasoned guide takes you on Upper Myakka Lake. The park has a campground for both tents and trailers, and five rustic, furnished cabins. Hiking trials, including a backpacking trail, and riding trails meander through the park, and rangers are available for guided tours. It's an ideal spot for bird watching.

THE TRAIL

The section of the Myakka accessible from SNOOK HAVEN isn't as awesome as other Florida canoe trails, but it's a pleasant, worthwhile, and easy ride up Hog Creek, past the mangroves, cabbage palms, oaks, tall river grass, and wild coffee and leather ferns. We

spot the resident 10-foot gator snoozing on the banks and watch in
awe as he opens one sleepy eye before he slithers into the murky, tea-
colored blackwater. Fish school in the shallows, and we see many
varieties of snakes, turtles, and birds. It's said that wild boar, deer,
and other wetland animals still lurk deep in the tropical underbrush;
a seven-foot shark was once caught on the river. Just a whisper of
traffic from I-75, muffled by the dense foliage, reaches us as we paddle on to the Myakka where there's more boat traffic. We find the
river is worth exploring, although there are many rustic homes on its
wooded shores. When we disembark once more at the camp, we feel
as if we've shared, for a little while, the quiet and solitude of the former territory of the turbaned Seminole Indians.

Later in the day, we slide our canoe into the waters of Myakka Lake
at the state park, and paddle across a portion of its broad expanse until
we reach the well-marked trails that lead into narrow, winding tributaries. Here, the Florida wilderness closes in on us as we glide silently
over the still, dark water. This is one excursion we advise you to take in
cooler weather when we hope the insects are hibernating. The narrow
trails with overhanging foliage don't allow much of a breeze, but offer
spellbinding glimpses of a more primitive way of life. Rabbits, deer,
and red-shouldered hawks are common to the area, and we see our
share of alligators. We check landmarks carefully because we enjoy venturing into the fascinating little byways to explore the grassy marshes
and sloughs. We do lose our bearings, briefly, experienced though we
consider ourselves to be, and resort to our compass. It's easy to get
distracted by the beauty of these surroundings even though the trails
are well marked. A rule of thumb is to keep right of the many islands.
Four hours of pleasant round-trip paddling past pine flatwoods, oak

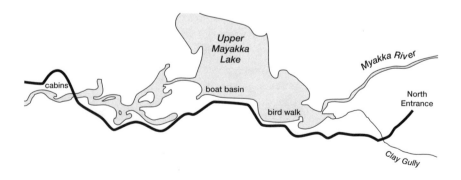

palm hammocks, mangroves, lily pad gardens, and river grasses provide an interesting and relaxing afternoon.

SNOOK HAVEN   MYAKKA RIVER STATE PARK
GENERAL RATING: XXX   GENERAL RATING: XXX
DIFFICULTY: EASY   DIFFICULTY: MODERATE
SCENERY: GOOD   SCENERY: GOOD

Myakka River

Myakka River

PEACE RIVER

With headwaters in the Green Swamp northeast of Tampa, this is an historic river whose west banks below Fort Meade were the site of one of the last skirmishes of the Seminole War. In 1842, an agreement was reached between crafty Seminole Indian Chief Billy Bowlegs and General Worth, establishing the river as a boundary between Indian territory to the east and white man's land to the west. Ignoring the terms of the treaty, and continuing to feel threatened, the restless Seminoles attacked the Fort, and a bloody battle ensued, marking the onset of the Third Seminole War. Phosphate mines once traumatized the river beds and the foliage, but the land has been revitalized, and now commercial intrusion is carefully monitored. Today, the Peace River, true to its name, is a serene, slow-moving river with little sign of civilization. On early Spanish maps it is called "Rio de la Paz," "river of peace." The Seminoles called it Tolopchopko (Creek of Long Peas), perhaps because the river banks were covered with trees whose leaves seemed to undulate.

CANOE RENTALS

CANOE SAFARI
3020 NW County Road 661
Arcadia FL 33821
(541) 494-7865
Susan and Dan Neads

CANOE OUTPOST
2816 NW County Road 661
Arcadia, FL 33821
(941) 494-1215
Charlotte and Son Bragg

Both liveries are located off Route 17, on Highway 70 West in Hardee County near the Peace River Campground. If you elect to travel I-75, take Exit 37 and travel east on Highway 72 toward Arcadia. Drive to Highway 70 where you turn north to county line road then turn east. Each canoe rental has concession stands, restrooms with sinks at which you can wash up, and changing rooms. Both also offer shuttle service to various points of embarkation, and the multitudes of racks of canoes assure that everyone can be served.

CANOE OUTPOST, which advertises its facility as the oldest and and largest outfitter in the state of Florida, opened its doors in 1969. The staff is friendly and efficient, and provides attendance in the form of a tall, husky young man who effortlessly handles the canoes. He's there to greet you at the end of the trip and help you disembark. Susan and Dan Neads of CANOE SAFARI, have a more rustic-looking operation, but it's just as efficient, and the canoes are well-maintained: paddles, seat cushions, and life preservers kept in good condition. You have a choice of five excursions, lasting from three hours to overnights. Back rests can be rented for $1.50, as well as ice chests for $6. Like most full- or half-day adventures, these canoe trails begin at 8 a.m. and close at sundown. The cost at both liveries is $20 to $22 (depending on length of trip) per canoe for all-day rentals. It's imperative that you check in at the office a half-hour before departure time, and it's always a good idea to call for a reservation. The livery is open seven days a week, closed Thanksgiving and a few days at Christmas. As in the case of the OUTPOST, attendants carry your canoe to the water's edge, help you embark, making sure you know the rudiments of the sport, and hand you literature describing the various trails.

CONCESSIONS

Both outlets include general stores offering varieties of snacks, ice, fishing equipment, souvenir caps and shirts, and sundries. CANOE SAFARI also advertises a free barbecue at SONNY'S the first full weekend of each month, March through December. The procedure is the same at each office: You check in, then hand over your driver's license (for identification in case of emergency). It's best to leave your car keys, too, and anything else you want to protect from possible spills. Bring your bathing suit if the weather is warm, but it's not one of our favorite spots for swimming. The water is murky and the bottom of the river is littered with cans and bottles at times, so use discretion. What we do enjoy is renting a handled sieve and wading in the shallows (where we can see the bottom), to hunt for sharks' teeth and other fossils. After your canoe trip, you can opt for walking nature trails, or visit THE CALL OF THE WILD WILDLIFE MUSEUM nearby (you can get directions at the offices). Internationally known sculptor HOWARD SOLOMON'S famous castle in Ona is only ten miles away. For a $5 fee, you can take a tour of the castle Solomon built out of discarded printing plates from area newspapers, and enjoy his quirky sense of humor as he guides you past his unusual artwork and sculptures. You can have a bite to eat in the

BOAT IN THE MOAT, a massive replica of a Spanish galleon, also built by the artist, complete with bar and "serving wenches."

THE TRAILS

The Peace River, advertised as "subtropical, beautiful, and the most uninhabited of all Florida State Canoe Trails," meanders for approximately 133 miles from a site near Bartow in Polk County down to Charlotte Harbor near Punta Gorda. Pleasurable paddling is limited to the 90-mile stretch between Fort Meade and the vicinity of Fort Ogden. Some of the most popular and picturesque segments originate in Arcadia, and are easily accessible to those who rent canoes. All the trips mapped out by the liveries head downstream. For solitude and quiet, pick a weekday, because the Peace River is one of the most popular and well-traveled rivers in Florida. It's barren cattle country here in Arcadia, you note as you ride the antiquated bus carrying you to your embarkation point, and it's hard to imagine "wilderness canoe trips." But there are scenic excursions for everyone, from a three- or four-hour, leisurely downstream paddle to a two-day safari, and overnight camping with primitive conditions like tenting, which doesn't interest us in the least. We do agree that the Peace River is ideal for casual canoeists like ourselves. It takes approximately three-and-a-half to four hours of easy paddling to cover a ten-mile span. Shortly after we start out, we spy a colony of young alligators sunning themselves on the bank, but they scatter and vanish underwater as soon as we approach. Dense forests and sand bluffs border the waterway for most of the trip, giving the illusion of being alone in the wilds. Canoeing these waters involves navigating occasional "rapids." (Pros would sneer at using that term for any part of the Peace River.) When the water is shallow, as it is on our trip, quick assessments and judicious choices must be made. The molded trunks of towering cypress trees, the colorful clusters of wildflowers, and the occasional sightings of hawks and other native birds, turtles, otters, and gators, make it all worthwhile. The CANOE OUTPOST operates a private campground called Oakhill (blue signs identify the property), and are for the exclusive use of OUTPOST customers. For those who prefer to eat at picnic tables, they are provided here. The highlight of our trip is disembarking to stretch our legs at the campground at the very moment an eagle swoops down through the trees no more than 20 feet overhead, its enormous wing span casting a shadow over us. There are plenty of white sand beaches for picnics, too, and if you want to take the time, you can fish for snook, bass, or perch. The large craters we see on the sandy river bottom, we're told, are perch gill beds. All in all, aside from an occasional clattering airboat, and a few river homes lining the banks, it's peaceful on the Peace River.

GENERAL RATING: XXX
DIFFICULTY: EASY
SCENERY: EXCELLENT

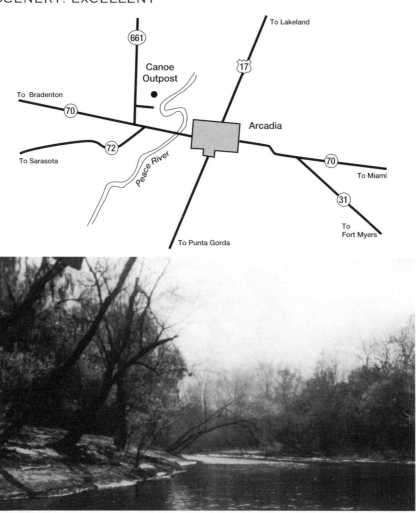

Peace River

SOUTH CREEK

The creek is located in OSCAR SCHERER STATE PARK in Osprey, just off the South Tamiami Trail (US 41) on the Gulf Coast between Sarasota and Venice. Although this charming little waterway apparently hasn't been accorded a mention in most publications on canoeing, it's worth exploring, and ideal for novices and children. Oscar Scherer State Park, like other Florida State parks, provides a habitat for many rare, threatened, or endangered plants and animals. The park was named after Oscar Scherer, an inventor who developed a process, in 1872, for dying leather used in the manufacture of shoes. In memory of her father, his daughter, Elsa Scherer Bowers, donated 462 acres of wilderness to the state of Florida for use as a park. The area was opened to the public in 1956, and, in 1991, another 922 acres was purchased, bringing the total property to 1,384 acres.

CANOE RENTALS

OSCAR SCHERER STATE PARK
1843 S. Tamiami Trail
Osprey, FL 34229
(941) 483-5956

The entrance fee for the park is $3.25 per vehicle, and canoes can be obtained at the entrance from one of the rangers. Rates are a mere $3.25 per hour, year-round, and the park is open from 8 a.m. until sunset. At present, cushions are not available, due to a limited budget, so bring your own if you need one. Since the concession stand has been closed because of a lack of funds, bring your own snack and something to quench your thirst on this short but pleasant paddle. It's the usual do-it-yourself state park experience, and necessitates carrying your equipment to the water's edge, dislodging the canoe from the rack, and launching it, so bring a companion who can help with this sort of exertion. We did see two elderly women managing the aluminum canoe themselves with little effort. Both canoes and equipment are in short supply, so call ahead to reserve them.

CONCESSIONS

Clean, modern toilet facilities and showers are located in the roomy, well-maintained bathhouse, and there's a pay phone outside. The numerous picnic spots, some sheltered, contain tables and outdoor grills. A small, freshwater lake with a beach provides excellent swimming, and there's a pleasant nature trail following the path of the creek. Fishing is good in South Creek with freshwater species above the dam, saltwater species below. A license is required as is the case with all Florida fishing areas. A camping area is located across the creek, and a primitive youth camping area is close by. Classes are scheduled in the picnic area to teach basic paddling skills and rules of the river. The park is near Venice and Sarasota, both of which offer countless varied recreational activities including the fabled beaches, boating, fishing, fine dining, golf, and good theater.

THE TRAIL

South Creek is an inviting waterway, surprisingly remote and still in the confinements of the park where powerboats are prohibited, along with firearms and alcoholic beverages. It's a pretty ride, accompanied by the musical calls of warblers and woodpeckers. We can paddle back and forth anywhere in the vicinity without fear of getting lost. Two plant communities are evident: the pine flatwoods, and the scrubby flatwoods, particularly noted for its prized population of Florida scrub jays. We don't see a bald eagle today, but they're here as well as bobcats, river otter, gopher tortoises, gopher frogs, and, it's said, the elusive indigo snake. Varieties of wading birds—in particular, the lovely blue heron—add spice to the trip. Today our nine-year-old granddaughter, Trecy, accompanies us, ensconced between us on the bottom of the two-seater canoe. Without effort, we paddle past slash pines, cabbage palms, mangroves, saw palmetto, countless wildflowers, and varieties of gnarled oaks. It's Trecy who spots the six-foot alligator, partly submerged at the water's edge, fearless and motionless as we quietly glide by whispering our delight. The river narrows as it winds its way under canopies of trees and creeper vines. When we reach the dam, we pull up to admire it, and to settle Trecy in the bow so she can paddle. She manages easily on the return trip, exclaiming over the joy of it. She's especially impressed with seeing the gator so close to the canoe. It's a two-hour trip if you stretch it out a little, and appropriate for adventurous kids who have a short attention span.

GENERAL RATING: XX
DIFFICULTY: VERY EASY EXCEPT FOR LAUNCHING
SCENERY: GOOD

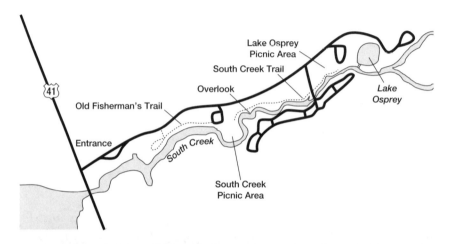

John Bergen and granddaughter Trecy at South Creek

TARPON BAY

Sanibel and Captiva islands are located in Lee County in the Gulf of Mexico across San Carlos Bay from Fort Meyers. The islands are world-famous treasure troves for shell seekers. Sanibel Island was inhabited by Native Americans, the Calusa Indians, for over 2,000 years until explorers and settlers took over. The J.N. "DING" DARLING NATIONAL WILDLIFE REFUGE, located on Sanibel Island, was named after one of the pioneers of the conservation movement, Jay Norwood Darling. "Ding" is the signature he used for his Pulitzer Prize-winning political cartoons. Darling headed the U.S. Biological Survey under Franklin Roosevelt's administration, and is credited with being a key figure in the establishment of the refuge.

CANOE RENTALS

CANOE ADVENTURES
P.O. Box 1332
Sanibel, FL 33957
(941) 472-5218

This livery is located on Captiva Island. It services Buck Key, and covers all the waters of both Captiva and Sanibel Islands.

TARPON BAY RECREATION
900 Tarpon Bay Road
Sanibel, FL 33957
(941) 472-8900
B. Coyne and Chuck Hoffman

You can reach Tarpon Bay Marina from the Sanibel Causeway (a $3 toll), go right on Periwinkle Way approximately three miles, then turn right at the Sanibel-Captiva intersection and right to Tarpon Bay Road, then a final right. The Tarpon Bay Recreation livery, which responded promptly to our query, is located near the edge of the bay, and offers canoes, kayaks, and sportboats with light electric trolling motors. A two-hour trip is available by canoe for $15, with a

$2.50 charge for each additional hour. Back rests can be rented for $1. The canoes are clean, easy to maneuver, and the attendants help you in, handing you life jackets while they recite the obligatory, basic precautions. You're handed a map that outlines the trail. We were cautioned to lather ourselves with mosquito and "no-seeum" repellent because, in spite of recent control, insects are still a problem on this barrier island even in cooler weather. You'll need sunscreen for the open stretches. The facility is open seven days a week, and hours are from 8–5, with the last rental available at 3 p.m. You can get a guided tour if you wish, but this must be reserved in advance. For your convenience, it's best to call before you drive down, to check on tides and choppy water. A tide table is provided by the managers.

CONCESSIONS

Tarpon Bay Recreation is one of the cleanest and best maintained facilities we've ever visited. In addition to an outfitter's shop fully stocked with tackle, T-shirts, caps, and other accessories, there's an espresso bar where you can start the day with your favorite cup of java especially prepared by a barista. Restrooms are especially clean and comfortable, and it's wise to freshen up there before you begin your trip as there's no convenient potty-stop along the trail. Except for taking along a snack and something to drink, we advise you to lunch before or afterwards on the wooden deck overlooking the water. The waters abound with redfish, trout, snook, and even an occasional tarpon, so take your fishing gear, or you can rent some if you'd like to try your luck.

THE TRAIL

The canoe excursion is located in a section of the J.N. "DING" DARLING WILDLIFE REFUGE on Sanibel, a subtropical barrier island composed of shell, sand, and silt. Dry ridges and wet sloughs now exist on this 12-mile long island fringed with mangroves, shallow bays, and white sandy beaches. It's November and the weather is beautiful . . . the beginning of canoe season, as far as we're concerned. Paddling these back-bay waters and a tidal creek through a mangrove forest, we observe first-hand the unique sub-tropical ecosystem. A fifteen-minute paddle over Tarpon Bay, the waters of which are often choppy, is the most strenuous part of this pleasurable canoe trip. Once we reach the inlet, there are no strong currents, and conditions are ideal for neophyte canoeists. The trail is well-marked all the way with blue signs, and we soon enter a narrow, crooked waterway that involves some tricky maneuvering, challenging our ability to navigate the many twisting turns. The utter silence is awesome as we pass nests of tangled mangrove roots, and occasional oncoming canoeists or kayakers. There's no loud talk or singing here. These are serious nature lovers like ourselves. The wildlife is abundant, and, depending on the season, you can spot ospreys, roseate spoonbills, cormorants, ducks, herons, and countless other species along with the hardy pelicans. We have our picnic lunch afterward on the deck before driving over to the refuge, a worthwhile trip offering a chance to observe alligators, and some of the 50 other reptiles and amphibians, at least 30 species of mammals, and 291 of birds.

GENERAL RATING: XXX
DIFFICULTY: EASY
SCENERY: EXCELLENT

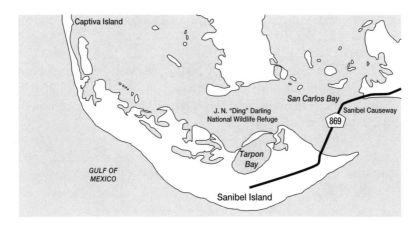

BIBLIOGRAPHY

Anderson, Robert. *Canoeing Florida,* Volumes 1, 2, and 3. Winner Enterprises, Altamonte Springs, FL, 1990.

Carter, Elizabeth F., and Pearce, John L. *Canoeing and Kayaking Guide to the Streams of Florida,* Volume I, North Central Peninsula. Menemsha Ridge Press, Birmingham, AL, 1985.

Carter, W. Horace. *Florida Nature Coast.* Atlantic Publishing Co., Tabor City, NC, 1994.

Florida Advisory Council on Environmental Education. *Florida Trails.* Tallahassee, FL (updated annually).

Florida Department of Natural Resources. *Florida Rivers Assessment.* Tallahassee, FL (updated annually).

Glaros, Lou, and Spahr, Doug. *Canoeing and Kayaking Guide to the Streams of Florida,* Volume II, Central and Southern Peninsula. Menemsha Ridge Press, Birmingham, AL, 1987.

Toner, Mike, and Toner, Pat. *Florida by Paddle and Pack.* Banyan Books, Inc., Miami, FL, 1979.

NOTE: The Florida Department of Natural Resources has access to innumerable publications, maps, newspaper and magazine articles, etc., designed to fit your specific needs. For information, contact the department at:

3900 Commonwealth Blvd.
Tallahassee, FL 32399-3000
(904) 487-3671

For additional information and services, contact the American Canoe Association and the Professional Paddlesports Association:

Jamie Leasure
7432 Alban State Blvd., Suite B-226
Springfield, VA 22150-2311
(703) 451-0141

INDEX OF WATERWAYS